Weston H. Agor, Ph.D., directs the Master of Public Administration Program at the University of Texas at El Paso, and he is also president of ENFP Enterprises, Inc., a management consulting firm. He has served in numerous top policy-making positions in business, government, and higher education and is the recipient of many human service awards and fellowships. Cited in *Who's Who in America,* he conducts workshops all over the country on how to develop and use intuition.

Intuitive Management

Integrating Left and Right Brain Management Skills

Weston H. Agor, Ph.D.

PRENTICE-HALL, INC., Englewood Cliffs, New Jersey 07632

Library of Congress Cataloging in Publication Data

Agor, Weston H., (date)
   Intuitive management.

   (A Reward book)
   Bibliography: p. 117
   Includes index.
   1. Management. 2. Intuition (Psychology) I. Title.
HD38.A317–1984   658.4′001′9   83-24554
ISBN 0-13-502733-0
ISBN 0-13-502725-X (pbk.)

Editorial/production supervision: Suse L. Cioffi
Cover design by Neil Stuart
Manufacturing buyer: Patrick Mahoney

Permission to use quotes from letters to author by Frances E. Vaughan, Alan Vaughan, Stephen K. Blumberg, and Charlotte Leibel reviewing this book prior to publication and in any subsequent publicity to promote the book or its sale.

10 9 8 7 6 5 4 3

Printed in the United States of America

ISBN 0-13-502733-0

ISBN 0-13-502725-X {PBK.}

To the women who taught me to feel:
 Ruth (my mother),
 Ruth (my surrogate mother),
 Dottie,
 Sheila,
 Eliana,
 Nancy,
 Margaret,
 Carolyn,
 Summerschild,
 Barbara,
 Marcia,
 Patti,
 Doris,
 Peggy,
 Ruthie (my love).
I love you!

Contents

"The potentials of the mind are awesome. Sometimes one feels lazy, frightened, and uncertain in the quest for self-knowledge. Sometimes it seems easier to play old games, to maintain old images, unsatisfactory as these may be, than to risk stripping away a facade and seeing who one really is. Because of this, the commitment to awakening intuition requires relentless courage and a continuing willingness to face the unknown."*

* Excerpt from *Awakening Intuition* by Frances Vaughan, copyright © 1979 by Frances Vaughan, reprinted by permission of Doubleday & Co., Inc.

Preface

I have often been asked how I got interested in the subject of using intuition in management. As a child, I didn't seem to have any special gifts in this field myself. I certainly couldn't bend objects, read people's minds, or demonstrate other skills often called "psychic ability."

In fact, my formal training as a child was predominantly left brain in orientation. I was encouraged by my parents and teachers to be sure to learn the traditional skills necessary for a successful professional career such as math, English, and Latin ("It will be very important in a law career you know!"). In a nutshell, I was encouraged to pursue the classic American dream—get the "right" education at the "right" schools, the "right" job, the "right" girl, settle in the "right" community, have two children, and live happily ever after.

I didn't receive much formal training in so-called right brain subjects or techniques when I was growing up either. Even when I was exposed to subjects in this area, the orientation was more one of, "It is something you must learn" rather than "What would you like to learn?"

Even though I didn't receive much encouragement to get in touch with or develop my right brain skills when I was growing up, I was always curious about such subjects as ESP. As I grew older, this curiosity was fed by a series of scattered events ranging all the way from seeing a famous mentalist work (Kreskin) to having the awareness that a close friend had died *before* I was officially notified that he had.

When I took my first full-time job after college (international marketing with Procter & Gamble), I became fascinated by a related phenomenon. Certain managers seemed to have an uncanny ability to know when to ignore the computer printouts and the financial analysts' advice when making marketing decisions—and be right! A few years later, I had the opportunity to work as special assistant to the governor of Michigan, William G. Milliken. Again, I encountered this same uncanny ability to sense intuitively how to make the right decision at the right time—even when information on which to base important decisions was incomplete or totally inadequate.

It was at this point that I developed a serious professional interest in the subject of intuitive management—that is, the ability to make practical management decisions successfully on the basis of feelings—even in the face of conflicting facts or with totally inadequate information. I studied everything I could get my hands on that appeared to be related to the subject, such as the pioneering book by Douglas Dean and others entitled, *Executive ESP*.[1] I attended seminars and workshops across the country on any subject that appeared to hold clues to understanding this ability, how it is practiced, and how it can be developed in each of us.[2]

This book is the product of my quest. I am going to share with you what I have learned so that you too can benefit from what I have experienced. In Chapter 1, I describe what intuition is and how it has been used in management to make day-to-day decisions successfully. I will also indicate how intuition is likely to become more and more valuable as a management tool in organizational settings of the future. You will also have a chance to test yourself. Chapter 2 outlines the results of testing I have done of more than 2000 managers across the country. In this testing, managers' ability to use intuition as well as other brain skills was measured in a wide variety of organizational settings (business, government, military, education, and health), management levels, and occupational specializations. Data were also collected showing major differences between men and women and between persons of various ethnic backgrounds. This chapter also shows how some managers have the ability to use intuition on the job to make decisions productively but fail to use this skill to their full potential. You will be able to see how you compare to these groups.

Chapter 3 describes step by step how you, as managers of organizations, educators, or trainers, can use the test findings outlined in Chapter 2 to increase productivity and job satisfaction at work and in the personal lives of your staff—and for yourself! In this chapter, you will see how brain skill assessments can be used daily in a practical way to manage human capital more effectively. Tools and techniques for assessing brain skills will also be described, and case study examples of their possible use in such organizations as Walt Disney Enterprises and Rockwell International will be outlined so that you can obtain a better understanding of the potential that brain skill assessment has for increasing productivity in your personal and organizational life. Special attention will be given to assessing the ability to use intuition to make management decisions since it is one of the key sources for generating the new and creative ideas that will fuel the organizations and managers of tomorrow.

Chapter 4 of the book will show step by step how you can work to develop your intuitive ability further and use this skill effectively to make the decisions you are increasingly likely to face in future organizations. The techniques outlined here have been developed as a product of successful workshop interventions with major organizations and top managers across the country. The last chapter of the book discusses some of the most innovative and pioneering work presently being conducted on the use of right brain skills such as intuition to make actual management decisions in modern day organizations. This chapter will also describe why many of these techniques and applications now being developed will be commonly used in organizations to increase productivity in this very next decade. It is also suggested that the systematic use of these right brain tools and techniques to complement the present emphasis on left brain applications in day-to-day decision making will hold the key to America's capacity to compete economically on a worldwide basis in the balance of this century.

Acknowledgments

As in any major project of this type, there are many people to thank for their assistance. Robert Ball of Coral Gables, Florida and Charlotte P. Leibel of Miami Beach, Florida, and Lilia Logette of Hollywood, Florida helped develop my initial interest in intuition, psychic phenomena, and related subjects such as handwriting analysis. Damien Simpson and Nicki Millette of The Universal Mind Science Church in Long Beach, California and The University of the Trees meditation group in Boulder Creek, California, kept my initial interest alive and growing. Betty Edwards, the author of *Drawing on the Right Side of the Brain,* gave me support when few others did.

Thank you to all the key people who helped write endorsement letters to ensure a high response rate to my questionnaire: Ray Goode, General Neil E. Allgood, David Pingree, "Bo" Donly, Bill Snow, Senator Robert VanderLaan, Dan Angel, Jerry O'Neil, Carol Lawrence, and Gus Turnbull III. Thanks also to the more than 2000 managers who responded. I couldn't have written the book without you!

Thanks to California State University at Long Beach for computer time and mailing assistance and the University of Texas at El Paso for secretarial support. Helpful assistance was also provided through comments on an earlier draft of the book by Dr. Steve Blumberg, Alan Vaughan, Francis Vaughan, Charlotte P. Leibel, Jerry Crecca, and my graduate students both in California and Texas. I wish also to thank the many others too numerous to mention who helped in various stages of this project. Special thanks to my typists, Florence Dick and Judy Gill, who helped keep me on schedule. Thanks also to Saul Cohen, Aquisition Editor of the General Publishing Division at Prentice-Hall, for bringing it all together into this finished product. Finally, thanks to "The Universal Mind" that selected me for this project, and guided me to its completion. I also acknowledge the work and encouragement of the late Ben Goodspeed.

Weston H. Agor
El Paso, Texas

1
Intuition as a Brain Skill in Management

Today organizations and managers basically employ three broad types of management styles for making decisions. (See Table 1.1.) The first, often referred to as *left brain,* has traditionally received the most attention in management education programs in both the private and public sectors across the country.[1] This style stresses employing analytical and quantitative techniques such as management by objectives (MBO), program evaluation review techniques (PERT), and forecasting to make management decisions. So-called rational and logical methods of reasoning are followed. There is a preference for solving problems by breaking them down into manageable parts, then approaching the problem sequentially relying on logic and data as tools in the process. Computers are the primary technological assistants used in this method. Management settings are normally highly structured, hierarchical in nature, and methods of decision making are carefully planned. Example organizations would be General Motors, the military, and many governmental units across the country.

An alternative and complementary management style employs *right brain* skills.[2] This approach, which has received considerably less attention and resource support in most of the leading management education/training programs until recently, stresses quite different techniques for problem solving. Here, reliance is placed primarily on feelings before facts when making decisions. Intuitive and inductive techniques are employed. Problems are solved by first looking at the whole—often with inadequate information or data at hand. Decisions are then reached through intuitive insights or flashes of awareness that are received. The management setting in which right brain skills are normally employed

1

TABLE 1.1. Brain Styles in Management

LEFT BRAIN	RIGHT BRAIN	INTEGRATED
Analytical	Intuitive	Uses left and right brain styles interchangeably
Deductive	Inductive	
Relies more on facts to make decisions	Relies more on feelings to make decisions	
Prefers hierarchical authority structures	Prefers collegial and participatory authority structures	
Prefers management situations that are structured and carefully planned	Prefers management situations that are unstructured, fluid, and spontaneous	
Prefers solving problems by breaking them down into parts, then approaching the problem sequentially using logic	Prefers solving problems by looking at the whole, then approaching the problem through patterns using hunches	

tends to be more informal and collegial. Participatory and horizontal authority structures are employed, and decisions tend to be made in a somewhat more unstructured, fluid, and spontaneous manner. Example organizations would be Apple Computers, Atari, Inc., Walt Disney Enterprises, and selected intelligence agencies.

The third style which has often been called *integrated* employs both left and right brain skills interchangeably as the management situation demands.[3] Managers who rely on this approach normally feel comfortable dealing with both facts and feelings when making decisions. They are "switch hitters" so to speak. But, they also tend to make their major decisions guided by intuition after scanning the available facts and receiving input from the management resources/personnel both on the left and the right in the organization. Frequently, the intuitive decisions made are in conflict with the course suggested by the available facts and forward projections based thereon. Example organizations relying most on this style would be such companies as Procter & Gamble, McDonald's, and Bechtel featured in the current best selling book, *In Search of Excellence,* as well as innovative public sector organizations such as Dade County, Florida.[4]

The use of intuition is a critical skill in both right brain and integrative decision-making styles. Until recently, the ability to make decisions using intuition received relatively little attention, and research on the topic is still extremely limited.[5]

This situation now appears to be changing rapidly. Recently, for example, *The Wall Street Journal* featured an article entitled, "How Do You Know When to Listen to Your Intuition?"[6]

Similarly, *American Banker* recently ran several articles stressing the importance of intuition in decision making including one written by Bennett Goodspeed, the late partner of Inferential Focus, a New York City firm that specializes in the use of inductive services for blue chip companies.[7] Numerous other management and popular magazines such as *The Harvard Business Review, Fortune, Success, New Woman,* and *Cosmopolitan* have also published articles focusing on the importance of intuition in daily decision making.[8] Even leading business schools such as Stanford University are now experimenting with new courses designed to focus on the intuitive aspects of decision making.[9]

There was a time when executives were reluctant to admit that they often relied on intuition rather than on facts and computer printouts to make some of their most important decisions. For example, when Douglas Dean, John Mihalasky, and others tested major corporate executives' extrasensory perception (ESP) ability a decade ago, they found they were willing to admit how they often made decisions only after testing showed that executives with the highest precognitive ability (ability to see the future) also had the highest profit record.[10]

Today, however, there is a greater willingness on the part of top executives to acknowledge that intuition is a critical skill that they rely on daily to make key decisions. They also acknowledge that intuition is a critical link to their success. Recently, Paul Cook, founder and president of Raychem Corporation, was asked whether he used much intuition in his decision making. Cook replied that nearly all of his decisions are based on intuition, and that the only major decisions he regrets were ones not based on it.[11] Robert Bernstein, chairman of the publishing company Random House, states, "Only intuition can protect you from the most dangerous individual of all—the articulate incompetent."[12]

Apparently, intuition is an integral part of Japan's recent business success as well. Shigen Okada, head of one of Japan's largest department stores, recently explained the reason for his company's success, "It was due to our adoption of the West's pragmatic management combined with the spiritual, intuitive aspects of the East."[13]

Why is there this sudden interest in intuition as a tool in management? In part, it is due to a growing dissatisfaction with the management track record of success and failure in the past as a result of relying almost exclusively on a left brain style of decision making. J. W. Marriott, Jr., president of Marriott Corporation, put it this way:

> New strategies will be necessary for business survival in the future. Too many American companies have developed into bureaucracies. Too many

decisions are made at the top, and action has been overwhelmed by reports and board meetings. Problems are overanalyzed to death in too many businesses.[14]

His recommendation is, "Hold strongly to a few single beliefs, a willingness to take a calculated risk, and have courage in your convictions."

A 2-year study of the American auto industry conducted by the National Academy of Engineering and the National Research Council, affiliates of the National Academy of Sciences, concluded "the United States automobile industry is in crisis . . . and something close to a cultural revolution is needed to make fundamental changes in productivity, product quality, and the role of the work force."[15]

But, this recent interest in intuition is also due in part to a recognition that an entirely new set of management conditions are emerging that are likely to place a greater premium on this skill in future decision making. (See Table 1.2.) As such futurists as John Naisbitt, Willis W. Harman, and Alvin Toffler have pointed out, we are entering turbulent times where the economic and political climate will be characterized by rapid change, crises, and major structural dislocations.[16] Technological advances will be astronomical. At the same time, as a recent study entitled *The Innovative Organization: Productivity Programs in Action* points out, employees at every level in organizations will demand a greater role in decision making. As a result, bottom-up and horizontal communication in organizations is expected to increase rapidly.[17]

Under these conditions, it appears likely that individuals aspiring to top levels of management will need to possess a greater degree of right brain skills, including intuition, than ever before. This is so because the top leaders of tomorrow are going to be faced with management situations that will be extremely complex. They will need to make decisions under circumstances where complete data bases necessary for left brain (linear, deductive) processing will not be available, adequate, or too costly

TABLE 1.2. Trends Restructuring Skills Required
to Manage Future Organizations

FROM TODAY	→	TO THE FUTURE
A centralized society		A decentralized society
Forced technology		High tech/high touch
Hierarchies		Networking
Representative democracies		Participatory democracy
Machismo society		Androgynous society
Institutional help		Self-help
Vertical society		Horizontal society
Top-down society		Bottom-up society

to gather in a timely fashion. Computer projections for the future have never been terribly reliable, even in the most stable of times, as a basis for making decisions.[18] They are likely to become less so in the future. Furthermore, top managers are going to need to reach decisions in a "high touch" manner so that subordinates *know and feel* they have played a key role in the process.

If intuition is an important management tool that is likely to become more so over the next decade, what is it exactly? How can it be used in a .practical way to help make decisions?

Frances E. Vaughan, psychologist and author of the recent book, *Awakening Intuition*, defines intuition this way, "It is a way of knowing . . . recognizing the possibilities in any situation. Extrasensory perception, clairvoyance, and telepathy are part of the intuitive function."[19] *Webster's Dictionary* defines intuition as "the power of knowing, or knowledge obtained without recourse to inference or reasoning; innate or instinctive knowledge; familiarity, a quick ready apprehension."[20] Carl Jung, the famous psychologist, identified intuition as one of the four basic psychological functions. (The others are thinking, feeling, and sensing.) He defined intuition as the function that "explores the unknown, and senses possibilities and implications which may not be readily apparent."[21] *The Metaphysical Bible Dictionary* defines intuition as "the sixth sense . . . an immediate apprehension of the spiritual truth, a wisdom of the heart that is a much surer guide than the head."[22]

In Western philosophy, intuition is defined by such authors as Spinoza as a "superior way of knowing ultimate truth without the use of prior knowledge or reason."[23] Intuition and reason are considered entirely different processes which yield different kinds of knowledge. In Eastern philosophy, intuition is regarded as a faculty of the mind which develops in the course of spiritual growth. For example, Lama Govinda, Tibetan Buddhist, considers the intuitive mind as being simultaneously one with the universal mind and with differentiated knowledge. It is through intuition that the essence of life can be understood.[24]

As a tool for management decision making, I prefer a definition of intuition analogous to Robert Assagioli's concept of the superconscious.[25] From this perspective, intuition can be seen as a spiritual journey. As we become more open to new and different experiences and aware of their meaning, our intuitive ability grows and expands to the point that our "subconscious becomes our conscious and our conscious becomes our subconscious."

What does this mean in practical terms? Frequently in life, we have an intuitive understanding of a person or situation. But, normally we are afraid to act on the basis of this instant awareness of our feelings. Instead, we fall back to the tape we have often been socialized to program, "You had better wait, gather more facts, get to know the person or situation better." So, we delay our actions and our decisions. Hence, we push our immediate feel for the situation or person into our subconscious for awhile. Until we feel comfortable through actual day-to-day life experience to allow our feelings to surface again to our conscious mind (for example, we work or live with a person for 6 months), we do not come to fully understand why we felt the way we did months before when we failed to act on our instantaneous feelings.

Intuition, fully developed, then, is a highly efficient way of knowing. It is fast and accurate. Our system will process a wide array of information on many levels, and give us an instantaneous cue how to act. We have the answer even though we do not understand all the steps, or know fully all the information our system processed to give us this cue. The more open we are to our feelings, the more secure we become through practice in their ability to give us correct cues, and the less we project our own personal desires and wishes for a particular situation or person to be other than they *really are,* the more efficient our intuitive clues will become.

Many leading executives have learned to hone this process to the point that they can rely on their intuition to help make decisions successfully. Inferential Focus (IF) is a firm which specializes in using intuitive analytical skills to spot new emerging trends for such blue chip clients as Morgan Guarantee Trust and Getty Oil. IF analyzes 180 diverse publications from around the world each month, looking for early developments that, properly interpreted intuitively, will give IF clients the lead time they need. At IF, using intuition to spot subtle changes that will give the clue to new realities has become a successful decision art. Bennett Goodspeed, the law partner of IF, describes how the firm does it.

> In order to gain lead time, business managers need to develop skills similar to the diagnostic process of medicine. To be good diagnosticians, businessmen need to develop the skills to deal with soft information . . . The process of change invariably starts with aberrant and unique events that, when appreciated, reveal meaningful relationships. By listening to experts and studying analytically derived forecasts, one is, in effect, seeking pat answers for complex issues. In reality, looking for certainty in a changing world is the wrong direction to lean, as one cannot afford to have a dogmatic view of a world that is in constant flux.[26]

Steven Rogers employs intuition along with analytical techniques at Tektronix, Inc. to enhance the design of industrial production systems. Ongoing, Online Production Simulation (OOPS) involves participants in team sessions where relaxation, future history techniques, and hand-drawn graphics are used to generate alternatives.[27] Sam Bittner, a businessman in Omaha, recently described in *The Chronicle of Higher Education* how he uses intuition to hire new managers.

I hired a new manager with unusual qualifications. He has educational background of history and English, holds a master's degree in foreign languages, and speaks French and German fluently. He knew nothing about the scrap-metal business. I gave him one week of instruction and told him to make mistakes . . . He has turned this into one of the most efficiently run metal industries in the Middle West.[28]

Executives appear to use intuition in a wide variety of ways to help them solve their daily problems. Regular work and practice with this skill has enabled each executive to find the way intuition functions most effectively for them. For example, some executives count on their intuition to give warning signs concerning an impending decision. Robert A. M. Coppenrath, president and general manager of Auh-Gevaett, finds "it seems to work better as an alarm, a warning system, than a trigger for action."[29] On the other hand, Richard Brown, former president of Towle Manufacturing Co., uses his intuition as a vehicle for staying closely in touch with whatever problem is at hand. "When following intuition, you develop a natural tendency to stay closer to the decision and audit it earlier and more often than in decisions based on hard reasoning."[30] Working with his intuitive ability over the years, William G. McGinnis, city manager of Crescent City, California, developed this formula for how intuition can be used to generate good decisions in his organization.

I believe that good intuitive decisions are directly proportional to one's years of challenging experience, plus the number of related and worthwhile years of training and education, all divided by lack of confidence, or the fear of being replaced.[31]

LEVELS OF INTUITIVE AWARENESS

Intuitive flashes come to executives on several different levels. Just as gifted psychics will vary as to the medium they are best able to work with (for example, physical objects, mentally, hand touch, etc.), executives also need to learn and experience which level works best for them. Broadly speaking, intuition functions on four different levels: physical, emotional, mental, and spiritual.[32]

At the physical level, intuitive awareness comes in the form of bodily sensations. Sometimes we have a strong body response to a person or situation when there is no apparent surface reason for doing so. We simply know something without knowing how or why. Recent research indicates that we can be influenced by extrasensory stimulus even when we are not aware of it at the conscious level.[33] Put another way, our intuition is telling us what our body already knows to be true.

If you are experiencing a very stressful environment daily, for example, your body is probably giving you numerous clues such as headaches or stomachaches. These clues may be translated practically into action in several ways: alter the environment, remove yourself from the environment, or learn through stress reduction techniques how to handle the situation more effectively for your own long-term well being.

At the emotional level, intuitive signals are transmitted in the form of feelings. Surely many of us have had the experience sometime in our lives that we instantaneously liked or disliked someone we just met. Just feeling right or wrong about a situation or picking up visual cues about a person are good examples. Two Houston psychologists, Cat Bennett and Margaret Covington, earn between $500 and $1500 a day assisting lawyers pick juries by employing this skill. Bennett describes one technique she uses that works effectively for her. "I watch faces. There's an old saying that the eyes are the windows of the soul, and I believe that. All I'm looking for is a juror who will be open, flexible, and sensitive. I don't stereotype people no matter what their sex, race, or creed."[34]

Thirdly, intuitive cues can come to you on a mental level. This is when mentally you see a pattern or order to seemingly unrelated facts that may not be obvious to your colleagues just yet either. Albert Einstein attributed his theory of relativity to intuition—a flash of insight—not to a product of painstaking laboratory experiments and work with objective data. Charles Revson, the founder of Revlon, appeared to be able to operate effectively on this level when predicting what the future consumers of his products would be likely to want.[35]

Finally, intuition can function on a spiritual level. At this level, an executive will come in touch with how his or her organization's acts are interlinked with all of humanity. At this level, one becomes aware of the meaning of the old biblical saying, "As ye sow so shall ye reap." Emphasis is on the transpersonal and the underlying oneness of life. Bertrand Russell put it this way, "Three passions have governed my life . . . the longing for love, the search for knowledge, and unbearable pity for the suffering of mankind."[36] At this level, one's perspective of life alters as one's knowledge of "God" becomes manifest. Ralph Waldo Emerson wrote in his 1841 essay "Self-Reliance":

> The primary wisdom is intuition. In that deep force, the last fact behind which analysis cannot go, all things find their common origin . . . We lie in the lap of immense intelligence. We are the receivers of its truth and organs of its activity.[37]

Managers skilled in the use of intuition tend to possess particular decision-making attributes normally not as readily prevalent among more left brain managers. Carl Jung's research into personality types identified these characteristics as follows:

- see possibilities.
- look far ahead.
- furnish new ideas.
- spark things that seem impossible.
- supply ingenuity on problems.
- deal with a complexity having too many imponderables.[38]

Available research also indicates that managers who do exhibit intuitive decision-making ability normally have a number of characteristics in common. They tend to be curious and independent. Usually, they set their personal goals in life by determining their own priorities rather than being overly influenced by the external expectations of others. More often than not, they have a good self-image and do not try to be all things to all people. They are inclined to ask why not rather than why and are oriented toward finding solutions to existing problems rather than creating additional ones themselves. Intuitive managers also tend to seek results from their actions and prefer an informal decision-making organizational style than one that is highly structured. Frequently, there is evidence in childhood that a single individual emotionally touched their life (a teacher or friend, for example), and helped them get in touch with their ability to feel and thereby use intuition to make decisions.[39]

Often, studies of intuitive managers also reveal that their intuitive ability expanded significantly when cataclysmic events took place in their life (for example, loss of job, heart attack, loss of loved one). At these times, they were more willing to consider alternative patterns of making decisions from those practiced up to then, more prone to discard emotional blocks to doing so, and, as a result, more likely to place a greater reliance on using their feelings to make future decisions as opposed to a predominant reliance on facts.

TESTING FOR INTUITION

Since intuition appears to be a skill that can be used effectively for making decisions in management, can executives be tested for this ability?

The answer is yes. There are a number of psychological tests and instruments today which can be used to measure your intuitive ability. Perhaps the best known is the Myers-Briggs Type Indicator (MBTI). Used for over 30 years, this instrument has a good track record for reliability and validity.[40] It measures several aspects of your personality including intuitive ability. After taking the test, you not only have an indication of intuitive ability, but also how you rank on a scale from high to low. The test results can then be used to determine how strong your intuitive ability appears to be when compared with other executives or organizations who have also taken the test.

Your individual and organizational scores can then be examined in light of how you function personally on the job, and how the organization as a whole appears to operate. It may be found, for example, that your intuitive ability appears to match nicely with the skills frequently required in your present position and/or organization. But, the score results may also indicate a mismatch for both you and the organization. Or, you may discover in the process that you have a high level of intuitive ability, but are not using it to make decisions on the job for a variety of reasons.

There are a number of advantages to using the MBTI to measure your intuitive ability. A considerable amount of research has been conducted recently correlating the MBTI scores with other well-known psychological test instruments such as FIRO-B (Fundamental Interpersonal Relations Orientation-Behavior, which measures emotional needs such as control, inclusion, and affection) and success in particular occupational specializations.[41] Furthermore, other work has been completed showing how MBTI scores can be used to predict likely individual management styles and organizational cultures in actual work settings.[42] Taken together, this test information can be used practically by individuals and organizations to effectively guide programs designed to increase productivity and job satisfaction.

As indicated earlier, individuals and organizations exhibit three broad management styles—left, right, and integrative. Intuitive ability is particularly prevalent and useful among individuals and within organizations that emphasize right and integrative styles. Tests also exist for measuring these management styles which can be used in tandem with intuitive scores on the MBTI for individual career, guidance, personnel, and in organizational development programs. One test developed by The Mobius Society with the assistance of E. Paul Torrance from the University of Georgia was published in the October, 1981 issue of *Omni Magazine*.[43] Over 18,000 individuals responded nationally. Responses were classified by sex, occupational specialty, and other factors. Preliminary findings were reported in the November, 1982 issue of *Omni*, and will soon be released in book form.

One particular application of intuitive ability is the ability to see the future. Experimental work is presently underway by a number of organizations to test this precognitive ability and put it to practical use in organizational settings. Again, The Mobius Society is leading an effort in this area. In October 1981 and 1982, they published two tests called Psi-Q I and II, which are designed to tap this ability.[44] Another organization, The Institute for Futures Forecasting, under the leadership of David Loye, is presently conducting a national test to measure the same ability.

Loye is seeking to find individuals who can predict such practical future events as inflation rates, economic performance, and election results.[45]

HOW DO YOU SCORE?

If intuitive ability and management style are important links to organizational success and individual performance, just how do *you* score? How do your scores compare with top managers and other executives who have taken the test across the country?

Take this test now. Then turn to Chapter 2 where I'll explain how to score your test. I'll also outline how you can use the results to help guide your career . . . and make other important management decisions you are facing right now.

Test Your Management Style*

Recent scientific research indicates that you use the two sides of your brain very differently. The left side appears to handle analytical and verbal tasks (deductive), while the right side specializes in intuitive nonverbal thought (inductive). You tend to depend on one hemisphere of your brain more than the other. This pattern affects how you go about doing your present job, your productivity, and the satisfaction you get from your work.

By completing this test, you will learn your personal style. (*It takes only 10 minutes to complete.*) This information will help you learn how to expand your present management skills, improve your present job performance, and guide your future career plans. Answer as *honestly* as you can.

1. I prefer to concern myself with
   (a) what we can be sure of—the well-established truths.
   (b) hidden possibilities, uncertainties, and potentials.
   (c) both sets equally.
2. If there are several things I must do
   (a) I'll probably attempt to deal with them simultaneously.

---

*First 15 questions in instrument, "Test Your Management Style," are from the *Human Information Processing*℠ *Survey*, copyright © 1983 by Scholastic Testing Service, Inc. and authored by William Taggart and E. Paul Torrance. Reprinted by permission of Scholastic Testing Service, Inc. TM-HIP Systems, Inc.

These 15 questions also appeared as part of the Mobius PSI-Q Test, which appeared in *Omni Magazine* (October, 1981), which was copyrighted © 1981 by the Mobius Society. Reprinted also with the permission of Stephen A. Schwartz and Rand DeMattei.

Questions 16–27 are reproduced by special permission of the Publisher, Consulting Psychologists Press, Inc., Palo Alto, California 94306 from the Myers-Briggs Type Indicator copyright © 1962. Further reproduction is prohibited without the Publisher's consent.

    (b) I'll probably pick one, complete it, then move on.

    (c) I'm equally likely to concentrate on one thing at a time or deal with several things all at the same time.

3. If I am presented with a task to perform, I tend to
   - (a) organize it sequentially.
   - (b) organize it by showing relationships among the components.
   - (c) have no preference between sequential and relational organization.

4. This statement best applies to me:
   - (a) I use time to organize myself and my activities.
   - (b) I have difficulty in pacing my activities to meet deadlines.
   - (c) I pace my activities to time limits with ease.

5. I work best at
   - (a) improving something.
   - (b) inventing something.
   - (c) both improving and inventing.

6. I am
   - (a) not very conscious of body language; I prefer to listen to what people say.
   - (b) good at interpreting body language.
   - (c) good at understanding what people say and also the body language they use.

7. I have
   - (a) a preference for thinking concretely.
   - (b) a preference for abstract thinking.
   - (c) no preference for either concrete or abstract thinking. I think both concretely and abstractly.

8. I usually solve problems
   - (a) logically and rationally.
   - (b) according to my feelings.
   - (c) with both logic and feelings equally.

9. When I am being given instructions, I
   - (a) prefer a verbal description.
   - (b) prefer a demonstration.
   - (c) am equally satisfied with a description or a demonstration.

10. While solving problems, I
    - (a) usually take a playful approach.
    - (b) usually take a serious, businesslike approach.
    - (c) am equally likely to take a playful or a serious approach.

11. I like my work (or classes) to be
    - (a) planned, so that I know exactly what to do.
    - (b) unplanned, so that I can concentrate on whatever I feel like doing.
    - (c) planned, but allowing me opportunities to change as I go along.

12. I respond more to people when
    - (a) they appeal to my logical side (my intellect).

    (b) they appeal to my emotional side (my feelings).

    (c) they appeal equally to my emotional and my logical sides.

13. I prefer to learn

    (a) through exploration.

    (b) by examination.

    (c) through exploration and by examination equally.

14. When I'm reading about something new, I'm most likely to remember

    (a) the main ideas.

    (b) facts and details.

    (c) both the main ideas and details.

15. I have

    (a) a preference for outlining over summarizing.

    (b) a preference for summarizing over outlining.

    (c) no preference between summarizing and outlining information.

16. Do you usually get along better with

    (a) imaginative people?

    (b) realistic people?

17. In doing something that many other people do, does it appeal to you more to

    (a) do it in the accepted way?

    (b) invent a way of your own?

18. Is it higher praise to say someone has

    (a) vision?

    (b) common sense?

19. Would you rather be considered

    (a) a practical person?

    (b) an ingenious person?

20. Would you rather have as a friend someone who

    (a) is always coming up with new ideas?

    (b) has both feet on the ground?

Which word *in each pair* below appeals to you more?

21.	(a) theory	vs.	(b) certainty
22.	(a) build	vs.	(b) invent
23.	(a) statement	vs.	(b) concept
24.	(a) facts	vs.	(b) ideas
25.	(a) concrete	vs.	(b) abstract
26.	(a) theory	vs.	(b) experience
27.	(a) literal	vs.	(b) figurative

28. Depending on whether you are a business or government executive, answer the appropriate section of this question.

For Business Executives

Occupational Specialty (*pick one*) and level of Management (*pick one*) you are currently in.

Occupational Specialty
(a) General Administration
(b) Financial/Budget
(c) Planning
(d) Personnel/Organizational Development
(e) Production
(f) Other (specify)

Management Level
(a) Top
(b) Middle
(c) Lower

For Government Executives
Occupational Specialty (*pick one*), level of Government (*pick one*), and level of Management (*pick one*), you are *currently* in.

Occupational Specialty
(a) General Administration
(b) Policy Program Planning
(c) Urban and Regional Planning
(d) Fiscal and Budget
(e) Management Analysis
(f) Personnel Administration
(g) Law Enforcement
(h) Health and Hospital Administration
(i) Other (specify) _____

Government Level
(a) Federal
(b) State
(c) Local
(d) County

Management Level
(a) Top
(b) Middle
(c) Lower

29. I like my occupation and feel it is right for me.
    (a) Yes
    (b) No
30. Is your sex
    (a) female?
    (b) male?
31. Ethnic Background. (Circle the *one* with which you most closely identify.)
    (a) American Indian, Alaskan Native
    (b) Asian American, Asian Indian, Oriental, Southeast Asian
    (c) Filipino
    (d) Pacific Islander
    (e) Black Non-Hispanic
    (f) Mexican American, Chicano
    (g) Latin American, Puerto Rican, Cuban, other Hispanic
    (h) White Non-Hispanic, Caucasian, European, Middle Eastern, North African
    (i) Other

2

Testing the Brain Skills of Managers

TESTING MANAGERS

During 1981 and 1982, I tested managers across the country in a wide variety of organizational settings (business, government, education, military, and health) at all levels of management responsibility and in various occupational specializations. My goal was to find out just how intuitive actual managers appeared to be, and to determine if there was any significant variation from organization to organization and by management level. I also was interested in determining whether intuitive ability varied by sex, ethnic background, and by occupational specialty. The answers to these questions appeared to hold important information that could be used practically by individuals and organizations to increase productivity and overall job satisfaction in a variety of specific ways.

Besides testing for intuitive ability, I also tested managers to determine which of the three management styles, outlined in Chapter 1, they *actually used on the job*—left, right, or integrative. My goal here was to see if managers were using the management style on the job *consistent with* their underlying abilities. For example, if managers scored high on the scale for intuitive ability, presumably they should be exercising management styles that would draw most heavily on this skill (right and/or integrative). If they scored high on thinking, the opposite end of the scale, presumably they would prefer the left management style which places heavier reliance on facts and analysis when making decisions. If the actual patterns were significantly different than expected, the findings might hold a number of clues as to how to redesign some of our present personnel (selection, recruitment) and organizational development programs to enhance the productivity (efficiency and effectiveness) of the organizations and individuals involved.

TEST INSTRUMENT USED

The test used to measure managers across the country is the same one you just took. It consists of two parts (*see* Table 2.1). The first part of the test measured the management style (left, right, integrative) that executives said they *actually used* on the job to make decisions. This portion of the test contained 15 total questions selected from the Mobius Psi-Q 1 Test which was published in *Omni Magazine* in October, 1981.[1] The second part of the test measured executives' *underlying ability* to use intuition to make management decisions. This portion of the test consisted of 12 questions selected from the Myers-Briggs Type Indicator, a psychological instrument that, among other things, measures your ability to use intuition, as

TABLE 2.1. Management Style Test

PART	PURPOSE	STYLE POSSIBLE	
1 (*15 questions*)	Measures actual management style practiced on the job	Left (L) Right (R) Integrated (I)	
2 (*12 questions*)	Measures underlying potential ability	Thinking (T) Intuition (INTU)	
Total test (*27 questions*)	Measures management type	L-T R-T I-T	L-INTU R-INTU I-INTU

TABLE 2.2. Chart of Test Results

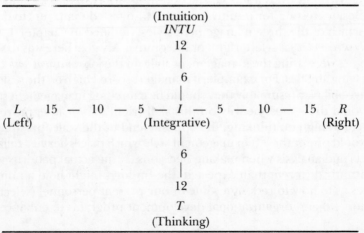

```
                        (Intuition)
                          INTU
                           12
                            |
                            6
                            |
  L      15 — 10 — 5 — I — 5 — 10 — 15      R
(Left)             (Integrative)         (Right)
                            |
                            6
                            |
                           12
                            T
                        (Thinking)
```

contrasted from thinking ability, to make decisions.[2] The Psi-Q 1 and
Myers-Briggs Type Indicator were selected as resources for constructing
my own test instrument because they have been used extensively to test
managers across the country, and have been proven to have a high degree
of reliability and validity as test instruments.[3] Scales were constructed for
both parts of my test so that each manager could be ranked exactly from
top to bottom on how they scored individually, and also how they compared to other managers taking the test. A maximum score on the first
part of the test is 15, and a minimum score is zero (horizontal scale). The
maximum score on the second part of the test is 12 with a minimum score
of zero (vertical scale).[4]

HOW TO SCORE YOUR TEST

Let's see how you scored now. Turn to your test answers and record the
results as outlined below. First, look at Part 1 of the test (questions 1
through 15). Total the number of (c) answers. This is your *integrative score.*
Next, total the number of (a) answers for questions 2, 10, 13, and 14.
Then total the number of (b) answers for questions 1, 3 through 9, 11, 12,
and 15. This combined total of (a) and (b) answers is your *right brain score.*

Now take the total number of questions (15). Subtract the number
you got for the integrative score *and* the number you got for the right
brain score. The result is your left brain score as follows:

15 minus (_____ + _____) = _____
                Integrative   Right Brain   Left Brain
                  Score   Score   Score

Summary: Integrative Score = _____

              Right Brain Score = _____

              Left Brain Score   = _____

Turn now to Part 2 of the test (questions 16 through 27). Total your (a)
answers for questions 16, 18, 20, 21, and 26. Next total your (b) answers
for questions 17, 19, 22 through 25, and 27. Together, your (a) answers
and (b) answers are your *intuitive score.* Since there is a total of 12 questions
in this part of the test, take the number 12 and subtract your intuitive
score. That number is your *thinking score.*

12 minus _____ = _____
                   Intuitive   Thinking
                   Score   Score

Summary: Intuitive Score = _____

           Thinking Score = _____

Take the response form below. This is the same form on which managers' scores were nationally recorded and returned to each executive taking the test. Read over the descriptive background explanation before you record your test scores as outlined below.

RESPONSE FORM FOR TESTING YOUR MANAGEMENT STYLE

Background

First of all, it should be emphasized that there is no perfect management style. Several styles of management can be productive depending on the organization, the mix of personnel within the organization (or under your leadership), your occupation, the particular task being performed, and other similar factors. Also important are *your own* personal career goals and aspirations.

　　Having said this, however, it is important to note that existing management research does indicate which styles/personal capabilities are more prevalent at the top levels of management/responsibility. Research also indicates which style is more likely to be productive and satisfying *for you* based on the type of organization you are with, your particular occupation, your job tasks, and your personality/capabilities.

What This Test Tells You

This test measures the *management style* you appear to use *now* (for example, the way you approach your tasks, people, and make decisions). It also indicates your *potential* ability to use intuition to make management decisions (which you may or *may not* be aware of). Your present and potential scores combined together is your *management type.*

　　The following is your management type and your *actual* and *potential* scores that make up that type. You will also find a description of how your results compare to other managers taking this test.

Test Results and Explanation

　　You are now ready to record your test scores. Part 1 of the test is your *actual management style.* Take your *top score* on this part of the test and record it below along with the appropriate capital letter (for example, I-7 or L-9). Part 2 of the test is your *potential capability.* Again, take the *top score only* on this part of the test and record it below (for example, INTU-9 or T-10). Step three is to record your *management type.* This is determined simply by taking the combined letters which represent your top scores on each part of the test (for example, L-T or L-INTU). If you have a tie score on either or both parts of the test, place an X in the appropriate space on the response form.

Your test results are:

1. Actual management style   _____
2. Potential capability   _____
3. Management type   _____
4. Most typical top management type   ___**I-INTU**___

You now know your management type. Graphically, you may want to record your scores on each part of the test on the chart of your test results section below.

Chart of Your Test Results

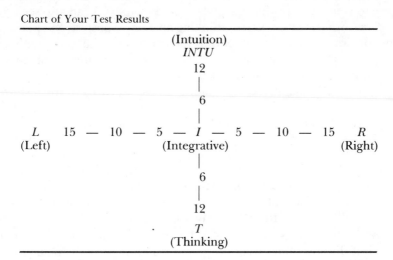

Now read the description that briefly outlines what your score actually means. Finally, you may wish to compare your scores with those for the most typical top management type as found in my national testing (I-INTU).

If your *actual* management style is L, it means you favor deductive, logical, and analytical processes to make decisions (for example, left brain). If your score is R, you favor inductive and subjective processes instead (for example, right brain). If your score is I (integrated), you prefer to use both left brain and right brain processes interchangeably depending on the task and situation.

If your *potential* capability is *INTU,* you have the ability to base your decisions on intuition (unknowns and possibilities). On the other hand, if your score is T (thinking) you prefer to make your decisions based on known facts and information.

If you have a tie score on either or both parts of the test, it is probable that you have difficulty deciding which cues to listen to and act on—the facts, your feelings, or both. This may also be apparent in the tension you experience when faced with making a choice between the cues you are receiving.

USING TEST RESULTS

The responses to these two distinct parts of the test together gives you and me a snapshot picture of your overall decision-making pattern. For example, I can quickly determine which management style (left, right, integrative) you *actually use* when making decisions on the job, and the degree to which you prefer that style over the others. I can also see *what level of underlying* intuitive versus thinking ability you possess. But perhaps even more importantly, by comparing and contrasting the score results on each part of the test, I can tell whether you are using the management style on the job that appeared *to match* your real underlying ability.

How can this be done? If, by the responses to Part 1 of the test, you indicate, for example, that you use left management style on the job, it means you rely more on facts and deductive patterns for making decisions. If, on the other hand, you scored high on the intuitive portion in the second part of the test, it would suggest that you are using a management style day to day that *does not match* your true underlying ability. This is analogous to pushing water upstream. One would expect you, as a manager, to rely more naturally on your *underlying strong suit* to make decisions on the job rather than the other way around.

When the management styles and scores on the first and second part of the test do not match well, these findings can be used to suggest a number of potential ways that an individual or organization can modify its present pattern of behavior which can lead to increased productivity and job satisfaction. As one illustration, suppose you, as a manager, score high left in management style on the first part of the test, and high intuitive on the second part. This is not the most productive match—it suggests that you are relying on your underlying weak side (thinking) to make decisions rather than the underlying strong suit in this case—intuition. More often

TABLE 2.3. How to Match Actual Management Style with Underlying Ability

MOST PRODUCTIVE MATCH	LEAST PRODUCTIVE MATCH
L-T	L-INTU
I-T	R-T
I-INTU	
R-INTU	

than not, this is due to the fact that you and other managers have developed a decision-making style early in childhood that may have been encouraged by family or other peers rather than being a product of natural underlying ability. It is probable that you would be more productive on the job if you altered your present preference for a left management style to either a right or integrative style, which more appropriately matches your actual underlying ability.

Similarly, because persons often develop a management style through formal family upbringing or training that may have little to do with their actual underlying ability, it is quite possible that people will self-select themselves to a particular specialty or job that does not match well with their real underlying ability. Often in cases like this, an examination of the manager's (or your own) health records, absentee rates, and other objective indicators (for example, do they enjoy their present position?) also serves as a warning sign that there is not the most productive match. These findings can then be used by the individual or organization to make the appropriate adjustments more likely to lead to both increased productivity and job satisfaction.

MANAGERS TESTED NATIONALLY

Now let's turn to my national sample of managers and see how they scored. Over 2000 managers have been tested in both private and public sectors. In selecting the managers to be tested, several criteria were employed. First, an effort was made to select managers from a wide horizontal range of different organizations and settings. This was done so that whatever the findings turned out to be, statements could be made more precisely about conditions under which the results appeared or did not appear to be valid in organizational life. Second, in each of the groups selected, an effort was made to obtain a representative sample of the total management structure so that meaningful statements (statistically significant) could be made from the findings about what the management style and intuitive ability was really like in each organization. Third, access also played a part in the organizations actually selected. In each management group tested, a major peer leader or top manager provided the necessary access to ensure that the questionnaire instrument was distributed and returned at a high rate.

The management groups actually tested were as follows. First, 5000 questionnaires were mailed nationally to a random sample of the public administration profession (membership of the American Society for Public Administration minus academics). Nearly 1700 (34%) questionnaires were returned. In addition, another 800 questionnaires were distributed to managers in a wide range of horizontally different groups (including

private sector chief executive officers (CEO's), emergency preparedness
military personnel, community college presidents, state health and rehabilitative services managers, city managers, and state legislators and
staff) representing three of the largest states in the nation (California,
Florida, and Michigan). Sixty-five percent (512) of the questionnaires
were returned from this sample. The response rate for all the groups
tested was so high because peer leaders wrote cover letters explaining the
test instrument and encouraged each manager to return the questionnaire.[5]

TABLE 2.4. Range of Management Groups Sampled

| | | RESPONSE RATE | |
GROUP	NUMBER SAMPLED	NUMBER	(%)
Private sector			
•*South Florida CEO's of*			
major corporations	88	54	(61)
Public sector			
•*National survey sample of*			
ASPA members	5,000	1,679	(34)
•*Three state sample*			
•Civil Servants	285	261	(92)
•Educators	100	43	(43)
•Military	50	44	(88)
•Politicians	110	47	(43)
•City managers	157	63	(40)
Total	702	458	(65)
Private and public sector samples	5,790	2,191	(38)

Responses were stratified by such key variables as level of management, level of government, sex, occupational specialization (using the
American Society for Public Administration membership classification
system), and ethnic background. All the responses were analyzed by
computer, and all the findings reported below were subject to statistical
significance tests. That is, are the differences found in scale scores between management levels, sex, occupational specialty, and ethnic background likely to occur *by chance*—or is it a measure of the actual differences that exist between these groups?[6]

TEST FINDINGS—TOP MANAGERS

The findings from this national testing are *dramatic!* Clearly, the dominant *styles* practiced by executives appear to vary by management level, by
level of government service, by sex, by occupational specialty, and, to
some degree, by ethnic background.

Intuition appears to be a skill that is more prevalent as one moves up the management ladder. Top managers in *every* sample group tested scored higher than middle/lower managers in their *underlying ability* to use intuition to make decisions (*see* Table 2.5). It also appears that the higher one goes in the level of government service (from county to national), the greater the ability to use intuition becomes (*see* Table 2.6). As outlined in Chapter 1, it appears plausible that one of the skills that top managers rely on most frequently is their intuitive ability to make the right decisions.

TABLE 2.5. Score on Intuition Scale by Level of Management

	Group Sampled				
	Private Sector	Public Sector			
Score on Intuition	South Florida COE's	National ASPA Sample		Three State Sample	
	LEVEL OF MANAGEMENT				
SCALE	Top	Top	Middle/ Lower	Top	Middle/ Lower
Maximum Score (12)					
High (8-11)					
Average (6-0)	6.3	6.5	5.8	6.2	5.6
Low (2-5)					
No Score					

TABLE 2.6. Score on Intuition Scale of ASPA Sample by Level of Government

GROUP SAMPLED	NATIONAL GOVERNMENT	STATE GOVERNMENT	LOCAL GOVERNMENT	COUNTY GOVERNMENT	TOTAL SAMPLE
(Number)	(441)	(414)	(595)	(229)	(1679)
Scale Score	6.7	6.4	6.1	5.9	6.3

Top managers also seem to be sharply different from their subordinates in the brain style they *actually use* on the job. An integrative brain style is most commonly practiced at the top levels of all organizations sampled. Comparing the results of both parts of the Management Style Test, we see that top executives practice overall an *Intuitive-Integrative Style* (INTU-I). They appear to work comfortably with both facts and figures and feeling for input into their decision-making process. But, when they are finally ready to act, top executives appear to rely more often than not on their intuition as their guide (*see* Table 2.7).

TABLE 2.7. Comparison of Dominant Brain Style Scores by Level of Management

	Group Sampled				
Score on Intuition-Integrative Scale	Private Sector	Public sector			
		National ASPA Sample		Three State Sample	
SCALE		LEVEL OF MANAGEMENT			
	Top	Top	Middle/Lower	Top	Middle/Lower
Maximum Score (27)					
High (13-26)		14.0		13.6	
Average (11.5)	12.5		11.7		11.4
No Score					

An Average INTU - I Score is 11.5.

These findings are consistent with recent research by David Loye of the Institute for Future Forecasting in California. Loye tested the ability of 135 subjects to forecast outcomes in the areas of United States politics, economics, and foreign affairs. He found that those who were most successful demonstrated an ability to integrate brain hemispheres on his hemispheric consensus prediction (HCP) test. Loye concludes:

> The current failures of economic forecasting by economists, a predominately left brain specialty, indicate the need for forecasting methods that employ more balanced brain usage.[7]

Donald A. Schon points out in a recent book entitled *The Reflective Practitioner: How Professionals Think in Action,* that in spite of the increasingly powerful status of management science and technique, top managers have also remained aware of the importance of what might be called *intuitive artistry* in decision making:

> In the last 20 years, "decision under uncertainty" has become a term of art. It has become commonplace for managers to speak of the "turbulent" environments in which problems do not lend themselves to the techniques of benefit-cost analysis or to probabilistic reasoning . . . Here they tend to speak not of technique but of "intuition."[8]

TEST FINDINGS—SEX DIFFERENCES

Another extremely important finding is that there are statistically significant differences between the sexes in management styles practiced by both private and public sector executives. Women consistently scored higher on the right brain scale for intuition than men in *every* group sampled. Women also prefer an integrative management style on the job *more than* men do. What may be most significant about this pattern of scores is the fact that women's overall management style appears to *approximate* that *of the top managers* tested more closely than men's style do (*see* Table 2.8).

TABLE 2.8. Comparison of Dominant Management Style by Sex

	BRAIN STYLE SCALE SCORES			
Sampled Group	*Intuition-Integrative (INTU-I)*		*Intuition (INTU)*	
	Men	*Women*	*Men*	*Women*
National ASPA survey sample	13.7	14.3	6.4	6.9
Three-state sample				
•Civil servants	12.7	13.3	5.7	6.3
•Educators	15.6	16.3	7.7	8.7
•Military	10.7	14.4	4.9	6.4
•Politicians	13.3	13.5	6.5	6.6

This suggests that, at present, there may be women in various levels of management who have the potential for top management responsibility, and that they can be identified, in part, through the use of tests such as those employed here. It should be noted here that this score pattern held up even when management level was controlled. The same was true within occupational specialties where intuitive and integrative skills appear to be particularly valued (for example, general administration and policy).

The fact that women score higher than men on tests measuring both ability to use intuition and to integrate cues coming from both hard and soft sources on the left and the right side of the brain is supported by other research that has recently appeared in such publications as *The Androgynous Manager* by Alice G. Sargent and *Discover Magazine*.[9] These studies suggest that women have learned to develop their native intuitive ability more than men have because historically they had to learn how to manipulate men in positions of power to get what they wanted. So as blind people learned to practice their other senses to the point that they could see color through touch, women have learned to practice and develop their intuitive ability. Simultaneously, men historically have learned behavior through societal and cultural pressure that did not encourage the development of intuition or other right brain skills (for example, men learned to suppress feelings and to rely on deductive processes vs. inductive). Some of the recent studies on male-female brain development also suggest that there may be different physiological patterns of growth that could help to account for score differences as well.[10]

TEST FINDINGS—DIFFERENCES BY OCCUPATIONAL SPECIALTY

It would not be surprising to find differences in management style by occupational specialty in private and public sector organizations across the country. Historically, certain professions such as management science, law enforcement, and financial management, for example, have emphasized left brain analytical, quantitative, and deductive techniques for decision making in preference to management skills requiring right brain skills such as intuition. Presumably, executives would also self-select themselves to that profession that emphasized the management style they also preferred or excelled in.[11]

At the same time, one might expect that as one moved from lower/middle levels of management to top management in *any* professional specialty, the skills required for successful decision making would change in character. Top management positions would appear to be more likely to require a greater capacity to solve complex problems, deal with uncertainty, motivate subordinates to act, and integrate factual information along with personnel needs, wants, and preferences into an effective management program that could be implemented. This job description would seem to place a greater premium on the ability to employ right brain skills such as intuition to make management choices.[12]

Available test scores do indicate that management style does vary significantly between occupational specializations and by management level within occupations. Take, for example, the occupational specializations of general administration and policy as compared with the specializations of financial management and law enforcement. We might expect managers specializing in financial management and law enforcement to have higher test scores on thinking vs. intuitive ability since these professions tend to place greater emphasis on facts and figures for decision making, value hierarchical models of management, and stress quantitative techniques of analysis. On the other hand, we would probably expect that the management style practiced most in the other two occupational specialties might place greater emphasis on right brain skills such as intuition. This is so because general administration and policy tend to be broader in scope. The issues a manager would be more likely to face would probably be significantly more complex. Elements of uncertainty and rapid change might be more common problems that would have to be dealt with along with a complex array of clientele groups demanding conflicting services. Intuitive skills in this context would appear to be particularly useful.

Table 2.9 compares the management style selected by executives in each of the example occupational specialties in question. You will note

TABLE 2.9. Management Style Practiced Most by Occupational Specialty for All Sampled Groups

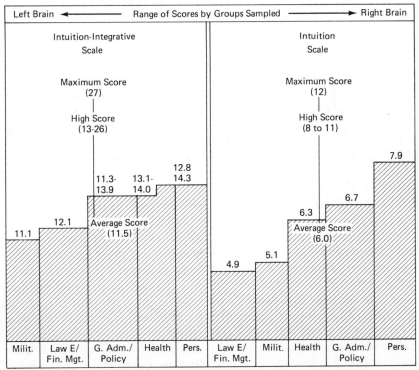

that managers in general administration and policy clearly prefer an intuitive-integrative style (INTU-I), whereas managers specializing in financial management and law enforcement prefer a thinking-integrative (T-I) style. However, as we move up the management ladder *within each* occupational specialty, you see that top managers tend to be more likely to place a greater emphasis on integrative brain styles as well as score higher in intuitive ability (*see* Table 2.10).

TABLE 2.10. Brain Style Scores Within Occupational Specialty by Management Level

SELECTED OCCUPATIONAL SPECIALTIES	BRAIN STYLE SCALE SCORES FOR NATIONAL ASPA SAMPLE INTUITION-INTEGRATIVE (INTU-I)			INTUITION (INTU)		
	Top	*Middle/ Lower*	*Total*	*Top*	*Middle/ Lower*	*Total*
General administration/ policy	14.4	12.0	14.2	6.9	6.4	6.6
Health	14.2	12.1	14.0	6.8	6.5	6.5
Financial management	13.9	11.9	13.0	6.1	5.7	5.9
Law enforcement	13.5	11.6	12.5	6.5	5.9	6.0
Total	14.0	11.7	13.7	6.5	5.8	6.4

Now this does not suggest that top managers in these occupations necessarily have an inherently higher intuitive ability at the outset than middle/lower level managers. This may indeed be true in part, but as outlined in Chapter 1, it is also probably due to the fact that these top managers have learned through practice to develop their inherent ability to the point that they can use it effectively on the job to make decisions. In fact, it could well be that managers, aspiring to top levels of responsibility in their respective organizations, need to learn to make this transition before their career goals can be successfully achieved.

TEST FINDINGS AND JOB SATISFACTION

One of the questions that was asked managers was whether they liked their present position or occupation. Nearly 6% of the respondents (over 100) indicated that they did not. When the management style this group said it preferred was examined alongside the occupations in which they were specializing, the findings were striking. The common thread throughout the data appeared to be that the vast majority of these managers had selected an occupational specialization that did not comfortably match either their management style preferences or their underlying native ability. These findings suggest that there is considerable opportunity within organizations for increasing not only job satisfaction but also productivity if these individuals could be *more appropriately placed* where their management skills fit more comfortably.

TEST FINDINGS AND ETHNIC BACKGROUND

Managers tested were also asked to identify their ethnic background. The purpose was to determine if there were any discernible differences in management style and ability. Since the vast majority of the respondents classified themselves as white, only two other groups (Asians and blacks) had large enough numbers represented to statistically measure whether significant differences were apparent.

The available data indicates that managers from Asian ethnic backgrounds appear to have a higher level of intuitive ability and are more likely to prefer an integrative management style than the average manager who responded (*see* Table 2.11). As has been suggested by Richard Pascale and Anthony Athos in *The Art of Japanese Management*, this could well mean that managers who were brought up in Asian family background settings were socialized from birth to emphasize and practice the Eastern world's approach to life which encourages the development of right brain skills such as intuition more than left brain skills.[13] One of the practical implications of these findings is that executives with Asian ethnic backgrounds could potentially be highly effective in management settings where intuitive skills would be at a premium (for example, crisis management, brain storming).

TABLE 2.11. Dominant Management Style by Ethnic Background

	INTUITIVE-INTEGRATIVE SCORE (INTU-I)	INTUITION (INTU)
Asian	14.7	6.5
Black	11.9	5.2
Total ASPA sample	13.7	6.4

Black managers, on the other hand, appeared to score somewhat lower than the average respondent on intuitive ability and were somewhat more prone to prefer a left management style, which emphasizes hierarchical authority patterns. Taken at face value, it would appear that black managers, on the average at present, would function best in situations where authority patterns are clear, and where the management task requires precision. Black managers aspiring to top management positions or occupational specialties requiring an emphasis on right brain skills could also probably benefit from workshop and training programs that would develop their ability to use these skills more effectively than they presently appear able to do.

PRACTICAL APPLICATION OF TEST FINDINGS FOR ORGANIZATIONAL MANAGEMENT

There are a number of ways that both public and private organizations *can practically* use these research findings to manage themselves more productively. First of all, organizations can use the broad findings here to help guide and enhance their present capacity to select and/or develop the right person for a particular position, occupation, or problem-solving situation. Our findings here strongly suggest that one of the factors to take into account is a candidate's brain skill/management style. (*See* Table 2.12.)

It would appear that searches for managers (either inside or outside the organization) *should emphasize different* brain skills/management styles,

TABLE 2.12. Management Situation Where Brain Style Is Most Appropriate

| LEVEL OF APPLICATION | THE THREE BRAIN STYLES IN ORGANIZATIONS | | |
	LEFT	INTEGRATIVE	RIGHT
Type of organization where predominant	Traditional pyramid	Dynamic	Open, temporary or rapid changes
Management style emphasized	Deductive Objective	Deductive Inductive used as appropriate and inter-changeably	Inductive Subjective
Example settings where most effective	Quantitative applications where data bases are available	Problem solving and labor management negotiations	Projection when new trends are emerging Crises Intelligence Holistic health
Example applications	Model building projection	Team building Synergistics	Brainstorming Challenge traditional assumptions
Occupational specialty	Planning Management Science Financial management Law Enforcement and the military	Top policy management and general administration Intelligence	Personnel Counseling Health Organizational development

depending on the management level, occupational specialty, and/or position in question.[14] For example, let us assume for a moment that an organization has as its prime task the recruitment of a new chief executive officer. Patterns to look for would be above average scores on a right brain scale testing for the skill intuition (INTU) and the management style intuition-integrative (INTU-I). This would be particularly true for organizations expecting to undergo a number of rapid changes in the near future. On the other hand, a search for a middle level finance manager or a director of computer services should probably stress a different mix of brain skills/management skills (for example, L-T or I-T). When searching for management positions that place a premium on right and/or integrative brain skills, our findings suggest that the search should include a careful assessment of candidates who are women and/or have Asian backgrounds.

Second, brain skill/management style assessment can also be used practically by organizations to *custom build* the most effective team or problem-solving group capable of addressing any particular issue requiring management attention (for example, assess the impact of technology on the future direction of an organization). For example, if one wished to create the management group most likely to come up with totally new approaches to solving existing problems in brainstorming sessions, weight should probably be given to R-INTU or I-INTU management types. (*See* Table 2.13.) If you would like to have a realistic assessment to determine which of the new approaches generated by that group could be implemented, it would probably be desirable to run them by a management team composed of L-T and/or I-T types.

Third, a brain skill/management style assessment program could be used as one vehicle for *identifying opportunities for increasing productivity* at both an individual and organizational level. This could be accomplished

TABLE 2.13. Management Situation Where Intuition is Most Useful

SITUATION	*METHOD TO USE*
Problem solving	Use intuition along with reason to come up with integrated solution that is both visionary and practical
Future projections Meeting crises	Explore alternative actions with limited or inadequate information at hand, pick the option that *feels* most possible and also practical
Team building	Use test results to build the team types that can best solve different problems at hand
Organization design Management	Use test results, work experience and own feeling to decide how to lead meetings, write memos, organize a room, communicate between departments, and pick personal staff

in at least three major ways: by diagnostic testing, matching of personnel with job specifications, and through training programs in brain skill development.

Through diagnostic testing, both the individual and the organization could have a clear assessment of the brain skills/management style capabilities and resources at hand. Gaps vis-à-vis apparent needs could also be identified through this process. For example, test results could be used to indicate what the individual/total organization's present and potential capability is for using left, right, and integrative management skills. You would also have an indicator of the *creative resources potentially available* through the scores on the intuitive portion of the test. This information could then be combined with other assessment tools (for example, review of resumes, personal interviews, past job performance) to generate specific targets for improvement in the present management of the organization.

One specific target could be realizing the best possible match between your personnel's brain skills/management capabilities and the job specifications within your organization. This could be achieved, in part, by taking into account the above test information by individual, and comparing it with the position each person is presently working in. This process might lead you to conclude that some individuals are poorly matched with the positions they fill. Another conclusion might be that the organization and/or the individual discover brain skills and abilities among existing staff that were not known. Maybe you will find that potential abilities are identified, but found to be presently blocked but subject to training. Still another conclusion might be that a search for different personnel outside the existing staff is required to meet the present/future needs of the organization.

Whatever the specific conclusions/actions generated by this stage in the program, training or retraining needs are likely to be identified for implementation. The goal of training would be for individual managers and the organization as a whole to achieve the most complete use of all *existing* and *potential* brain skills possible. First of all, the individual managers would need to be made fully aware of their existing and potential brain skills through a review of the results of the diagnostic testing program outlined above.

One of the features of the Management Style Test used in this study is that it measures *both* a person's *potential* capacity and *actual* usage of left, right, and integrative brain skills and styles. Nearly 6% of the managers tested appeared to possess the potential ability to use intuition to make decisions, for example, but indicated by their scores on the balance of the test (and in interviews in many cases) that they were either not relying on/or were reluctant to use this skill on the job. These managers would appear to be prime candidates for training programs designed to unblock potential right brain skills, such as intuition, so that they could be *actualized* to make decisions more productively.

The next step in training would be to demonstrate on an individual, group, and organizational level how more systematic use and matching of individual brain styles to organizational problems and occupational specializations and job specifications could lead practically to greater productivity and individual job satisfaction. Once each manager became fully aware (cognitively and affectively) of the direct relationship between more complete brain skill usage and organizational/personal goal fulfillment, he or she would become capable of working systematically on developing his or her own existing and potential brain skills more completely. For example, managers desiring or requiring more complete left brain skill development (deductive reasoning and analytical ability) could be channeled to particular courses, workshops, or clinics where this would take place. For managers seeking to learn how to develop their right brain skills (for example, intuition) and to apply them to solve real problems facing them in organizational settings, they would be similarly channeled to programs where these skills could be more fully developed and actualized. Likewise, those managers seeking to develop integrative brain skills (the use of left and right brain skills interchangeably) would be exposed to training tools to help them accomplish this objective.

In the next chapter, we will show you step by step how individual managers and organizations can implement brain skill programs so that productivity and job satisfaction can be significantly increased. We will also outline how selected major organizations such as Walt Disney Enterprises and Rockwell International could potentially use brain style assessments of their professional and management staff to design programs to improve their overall effectiveness.

3

How to Use Brain Skill
Assessments to Increase
Organizational Productivity

Every organization is faced with a common set of problems on a daily basis. A central issue is how to achieve maximum productivity (effectiveness and efficiency) at the least possible cost. If survival depends on productivity, it, in turn, depends on an organization or individual manager's ability to answer correctly a number of constantly unfolding questions. What will the future look like? What kind of resources (human and physical capital) will be needed to survive in this future scenario? How should they be organized and distributed?

Each organization and individual manager presently addresses these and other questions in a variety of ways using various management styles and techniques. This chapter will outline step by step how brain/management style programs can also be used toward this end. Case study examples of how some leading organizations and successful managers have implemented elements of these programs will also be presented here.

HUMAN CAPITAL MANAGEMENT

Human capital is potentially the most important source an organization has for its present and future survival. It is the source for creative solutions for existing problems, and the fountain from which new products and programs will flow. Human capital is also one of the most significant costs in organizational life today. In the public sector, it is usually the major cost item in governmental budgets having the most significant political implications. Yet, even though elaborate personnel and organizational development programs have emerged over the last decade in both the public and private sectors, the productive use of human capital skill remains a relatively rustic art. Basic questions such as, "What is the creative potential in the organization?" and "Where is it located?" and "How can it be developed and channeled for the common success of the organization and individuals involved?" go unanswered.

Using Brain Skill/Management Style Programs

Brain skill/management style (BMS) programs can be used in a variety of ways to help increase the productivity of human capital in organizations. At the outset, it is important to recognize that *job satisfaction* for an individual within the organization (whatever the level of management) is an important key to productivity. It is also important to recognize that organizations will *need to learn how to turn this key in the future* as employee demands increase for meaningful participation in decision making, as communications become more horizontal in decision making, and as decisions become more decentralized.[1] If a person *feels* unsatisfied (irrespective of the apparent indicators to the contrary), it is likely that the individual is not performing at maximum potential for his or herself—or for the organization. *Both* the individual and the organization are the losers. Satisfaction on the job is not a simple matter to assess. A number of objective indicators have been used in the past such as job performance, absentee rates, turnover, destruction on the job, and interviews. As you will see in a moment, brain skill assessment can also be used to complement and make present assessment efforts more effective.

Motivation is another side of the same coin. Even if an organization can identify that a person appears to be dissatisfied with his or her work, developing a program that will meet both the person's and organization's needs can be a difficult task. Again, we will see that a program of brain skill/management style assessment can be an effective complement to existing efforts toward this end.

Those managers responsible for the leadership of their organizations are faced with the difficult task of achieving maximum human capital productivity which, in turn, requires a greater and greater understanding of what is required to satisfy and motivate their colleagues and subordinates to perform. This, in turn, requires an understanding of just *who* these people are—that is, determining their skills, attributes, styles, and preferences. It also requires some assessment of what their potential ability and actual performance can be. Again, a program of brain skill/ management style assessment including training can be helpful in this regard.

A brain skill/management style (BMS) program can also be used practically to increase productivity by solving a wide array of other human capital management problems that organizations normally face on a regular basis. Some selected examples are listed in the table below.

TABLE 3.1. Typical Human Capital Management Problems
Where Brain Skill Programs Can Increase Productivity

- Recruit, place, and develop personnel by management level and occupational specialty including career changes, adaptation to organizational changes such as mergers, outplacement.
- Create teams that can solve problems on a situational basis (for example, crisis, intelligence).
- Assess future trends and implications for management.
- Assess, locate, and develop creative potential in organizations.
- Generate and make a practical assessment of creative ideas and/or new policy proposals.
- Understand and overcome communication problems including sex role stereotypes and cultural differences.
- Assess and manage stress.
- Develop and implement training programs.
- Develop workable employee compensation and benefit programs.

"Okay," you say, "it sounds intriguing and plausible. But, tell me specifically how a BMS program can work in reality. Give me some examples." One of the very first questions to ask yourself as a manager is, does my organization have an overall human capital management program? This doesn't mean simply having a personnel department that selects people to fill vacant positions or periodic *ad hoc* training programs so that people know the basics about the positions they just filled. It means having a *coherent overall plan* of how to use and develop human capital to achieve the organization's goals. Properly structured, the implementation of this plan will also lead to the achievement of the goals that individuals have for themselves professionally within their organization.

If your organization does not have such a plan at present, you have a *very significant* opportunity to increase productivity by designing and implementing one. Whether you are developing a plan from scratch—or assessing the one you presently have—one of the most important first steps is to assess the human capital you presently have. This assessment will give answers to such key questions as: Do I have the human capital resources necessary to achieve organizational goals at present (actual or potentially)? Are my resources located in the organization where they are or can be most productive? Is my employee compensation/benefit program effective?

Brain skill/management style assessment (BMS) can substantially increase the productivity of existing tools and techniques used in your organization toward this end. Take the example of Walt Disney Enterprises (WED) in 1982. This division of the Disney organization is the creative developer of theme parks such as Walt Disney World and EP-COT. WED had become one of the most profitable divisions in recent years, but professional and management staff had swelled from 600 to 2000 or so as work was being completed on the EPCOT Center in Orlando, Florida. WED was faced with a major management problem—now that EPCOT had been opened (fall, 1982), who should be retained, transferred to other divisions of the Disney organization, or let go outright? At the same time, WED was not yet clear on what its own future organizational goals should be and, thereby, what the staffing requirements might be. Clearly WED needed to establish long-range goal objectives and a new human capital management program before decisions could most productively be made in the interest of both WED and the staff concerned.[2]

In a situation like this, BMS assessments can be used practically to custom design the teams within WED that are best able to generate new organizational goals and objectives that can be realistically implemented. One outcome of such an assessment might be that such in-house teams should be complemented with input from outside the organization in order to help assure that all the plausible options are adequately considered. BMS assessments can also be used here to guide the development of an overall human capital management program capable of productivity matching the organizational goals just generated with specific programs for reaching them. This matching process can then be used to guide decisions concerning the staffing questions WED faced above. For example, one conclusion from this process might be that all the existing staff will be required to meet future WED goals. Another option can be that a reduction is required, and that some of the staff retained needs to be relocated and/or retrained.

Take another typical situation where BMS assessments can be used to guide management decisions. An employment supervisor of a large division of General Telephone and Electronics (GTE) in the Southwest needed to recruit a large number of engineers in a short period of time. Her division is growing rapidly, but she was finding that her assistant manager was not getting the job done successfully. Prime candidates enthusiastically came in for interviews with him, but seemed to often leave uninterested. She talked with her subordinate about the matter, and he seemed genuinely concerned about his performance. He even agreed to seek a professional outside assessment of the situation. This included among other things a BMS inventory. The conclusion was startling! The skills and management style required for this position did not match well with those of the assistant manager. For several years now, this individual had been trying to force himself into a job that he was not well suited for—nor really liked. Both the organization and the individual suffered as a result.[3]

Frequently, BMS assessments can be used to make executives conscious of how their management styles can be improved in a way that will help ensure the success of their organization. Recently, the president of a large cooperative grocery business reflected on the results of his BMS assessment. It showed that generally he had not encouraged input from his subordinates. "You know," he said, "I need input from my staff. I recognize now that I structured our meetings in a way that they didn't feel comfortable giving me new proposals or ideas. I'd shoot them down just as soon as they opened their mouths." He stopped for a moment with tears in his eyes. "You know, it takes a big man to talk about feelings like this."[4]

Recently, at a workshop with the organizational development staff of Rockwell International in Downey, California, one of the staff seemed extremely close-minded about the prospects of using BMS assessments practically in her organization. Before the presentation had begun, her mind was made up. As it turned out, she was an upwardly mobile woman intent on demonstrating that she was competent to her colleagues. As with many women in circumstances similar to hers these days, she thought adopting a style that was more macho than the machos was the way to accomplish her objective. In short, she was using extreme left brain approaches (highly critical, unimaginative) in a situation and manner where they were not functional or appropriate. When her own personal BMS assessment revealed that her underlying potential style was significantly different from the style she was actually employing to make decisions on the job, she suddenly became aware of the gap between the results on the two parts of the test which measured her management style. She wrote later:

> I was very impressed with the content of your presentation on Friday, and I was touched by your personalization of the content. Part of my job here at Rockwell is to do a needs analysis for an advanced management series. Rattling around in my brain is how we might use the test of management styles as part of that analysis.[5]

Resources for Conducting BMS Assessments[6]

BMS assessments can be conducted independently, or preferably as part of an overall human capital management program where other evaluation tools and techniques are also used. Assessments can be made for individuals, departments or divisions of an organization, or for the organization as a whole. Comparisons can also be made between these units. Assessments can also be used to deal with issues of communication between individuals, divisions or organizations, or between organizations themselves.

BMS assessments can rely on one, two, or an array of several test instruments and other measurement techniques depending on your goals and objectives. If a broad general assessment is all that is required, only one or two measurement instruments may be sufficient to give you the information you need. A good rule of thumb is the following: The more precise and detailed the assessment required, the wider array of instruments and techniques you should rely on.

The field testing of managers reported in this book employed only one BMS instrument, Test Your Management Style, which is the same test you took. The reason is that only a broad general picture of the management profession across the country was required at this stage for the purposes of the study. Also, the instrument used was based on elements of other tests which had a good record of reliability and validity. Therefore, this instrument is recommended as a first step in your personal or organization's BMS assessment.

This instrument can be used to get a broad overall picture of the personal brain style you use on the job day to day to make decisions. It can also give you an assessment of the level of intuitive or thinking ability you have in both absolute scale terms and also as compared with average management scores nationally—by management level, sex, ethnic background, and occupational specialty. You can also use these broad findings on each part of the test to obtain initial indication as to whether you appear to be *aligned*. These findings help determine if your style on the job is consistent with your underlying potential, and if your management style seems to match well with the skills required for your present position.

You may also wish to compare the findings of your BMS assessment with other information about yourself (or your personnel) that you have at hand. For example, check your own feelings. Do you like your job? If not, your BMS results may reveal why. Similarly, you may have taken other tests that, along with your employment history and health record, give a broad picture of who you are as an individual and as a manager. These same steps can be used to form a composite picture of an organization or parts thereof for assessment purposes.

At this stage, you may have adequate information for the purposes of your analysis. If so, stop. If, on the other hand, you feel you have some broad indicators of the direction in which you wish to go, but you feel you need much more precision and/or collaborating evidence before you can make a decision, proceed to the next step. This process may be compared to searching for oil. At the outset, you may only wish to know generally where to drill, and you may even drill a few test holes. With this additional information, you then select the site for concentrated exploration.

Once you have decided to proceed to this stage, there is a wide array of instruments you can use for more in-depth probes and analysis. One very useful instrument is the full Myers-Briggs Type Indicator. Consisting of 166 total questions, the instrument gives you a left-right brain skill assessment along four distinct scales including intuition-sensing. The score results can be classified into 16 distinct personality types that give a quite detailed indication of not only your skills and abilities, but also how you are likely to act in an organizational setting depending on the situation. Another advantage of this instrument is that a number of instructional aids have been prepared and are now available for use in management training programs.

Another instrument that would be useful at this stage is the full series of the Mobius Psi-Q Tests I and II. The first test consists of questions that measure not only left, right, and integrative brain styles on the job, but also assess precognitive ability (ability to see the future). The second tests ability to see the future using remote viewing techniques. A third instrument that may be helpful here is the FIRO-B developed by Will Schutz. This test, which consists of 54 questions, assesses your need structure along six dimensions—expression or want of inclusion, control, or affection. The particular pattern of scores received again can be used to assess how you are likely to function in an organization situation, and the scores can also serve, along with the other test results, to give a more detailed composite picture of your brain skills and management styles.

There are a number of other instruments and techniques that might be considered for use to get a more detailed picture of your own and/or your organization's human capital attributes and potential. Which of these tools you rely on, again, largely depends on your particular goals and objectives for conducting this assessment. A number of firms have good instruments available for use. One firm, Consulting Psychologists Press in Palo Alto, California, has a very large selection of test instruments including the Myers-Briggs Type Indicator and the FIRO-B previously mentioned. A recent addition to these offerings available from University Associates in San Diego, California, is a new set of instruments developed by Will Schutz that measures five different aspects of a manager's awareness: behavior, feelings, self-concept, relationships, and job. This assessment can be effectively used to indicate how a person is likely to function in an organizational setting and also to suggest the potential the person has for future training and development along these dimensions. The recently developed instruments in neuro-linguistic programming can also be considered.[7]

Human Synergistics in Plymouth, Michigan has prepared a series of exercises that can also be used in training sessions to show how BMS assessments will affect the way an individual or group is likely to go about solving an organizational problem, and how productive they will be in doing so. Many organizations also now employ handwriting analysts to determine a person's BMS patterns. Charlotte Leibel, a well-known handwriting analyst, has written a book entitled *Change Your Handwriting, Change Your Life,* which was recently reported in *New Woman Magazine.*[8] This book outlines how you can use handwriting to assess a broad range of capabilities including intuition, analytical skills, and management styles. She also describes how a person can go about changing present patterns of behavior as well as how to develop particular skills and attributes that one possesses to a greater degree.

HOW TO CONDUCT AND USE BMS ASSESSMENTS

Let's go step by step through a BMS assessment and show you how some of the instruments mentioned above can be used to manage human capital more productively. We noted earlier in the chapter that a key to individual and organizational productivity is job satisfaction. One of the most effective ways to achieve job satisfaction is to first learn *who your personnel are.* What are their skills and abilities? How do they think? What are their needs? This information can then be used to achieve organizational goals most productively by ensuring that individual goals and needs *are known,* and *then matched well* with organizational needs and tasks.

A Simulated BMS Assessment at Walt Disney Enterprises*

Here are some ways this can be accomplished. First, let's take the example of Walt Disney Enterprises again. Let's assume that you are president. You know that the Walt Disney organization as a whole is following WED closely. This is particularly true of late because the theme parks that you create and produce have become the major source of company revenue (69%), while films and television have declined sharply to now only 17% of the total. The size of your professional/management staff has grown rapidly in recent years (more than 300%), and many are relatively new at their jobs. Because of this rapid expansion, you are not entirely sure if they are all well placed or as productive as they could be. You are also concerned that you may not have always retained the personnel you wanted to. You recognize that WED's goals and objectives need to be totally reassessed now that EPCOT has successfully been opened, and this review will be a key factor in determining staffing requirements in the 1980s. You would also like to get an assessment of the communication patterns within WED. You sense they could be more productive and that there is room for improvement. You are particularly concerned about the ways the operating divisions interact and the patterns between manage-

---

*This is only a simulation exercise that illustrates how BMS assessments could potentially be conducted at WED. However, it should be emphasized that such company-wide assessments have not actually been conducted on a formal basis to date.

ment levels and between men and women on staff. This is so because conflict has erupted openly on several occasions between the production and administrative divisions over policy direction and allocation of resources. Also, some of the women managers wonder aloud whether the door is open to them at the top of the management team.

You wish to go about assessing your present professional/management staff. You have several goals in mind. First, you would like to get an overall snapshot picture of the organization's total human capital resources. Second, you would like to get a picture at the divisional and individual level. Third, you would like to be able to determine whether the current professional/management staff appears to be well placed *vis-à-vis* the duties they have to perform. As part of this process, you would also like to get an assessment of who appears to have high potential for future development that should be cultivated by the organization. You would like to know also who appears to have low potential and perhaps outplaced. Next, you would like to be able to determine ways in which communication can be improved within WED at various levels of the organization. Finally, you would like to be able to identify a group within the current management staff who would be most likely to be able to address the issue of what WED's long-term goals should be over the next decade. You would also like to know if this can be accomplished entirely within WED, or whether you need to also employ outside resources to handle this particular task.

You already have some key information on your professional/management staff in their personnel files. This consists of resources, evaluation of job performance, and other related information. This data alone can be helpful as a broad guide for getting the answers to the questions you have raised. However, the addition of BMS assessments can make this process far more productive for WED and the individuals involved.

Tests throughout the organization using the Test Your Management Style instrument reveal the following patterns. WED management as a whole is typified by an I-INTU management style which is similar to other top managers across the country. This means that managers are able to integrate facts and feelings effectively on the job to make decisions. It also appears that they have the capacity to rely on intuition more than facts to guide their decisions. What is particularly important to note is that WED management appears to have the potential to be far more creative in generating new ideas and concepts than is true of the average manager nationally. This can be seen in Table 3.2 by the fact that both their intuition and integration scores are substantially above the national average. In short, it would appear that WED has been successful in attracting the kind of management staff required for the type of business you are in.

Test results also indicate significant variation within WED. In some cases, this variation is consistent with national data that show variation by

TABLE 3.2. Comparison of WED Management to Average Top Managers Nationally
Scale Scores

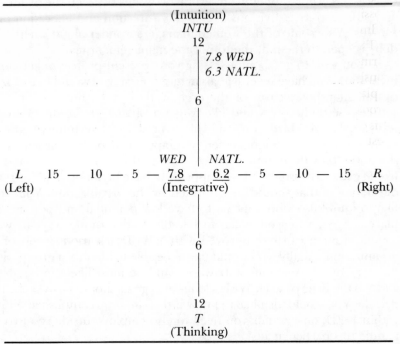

```
                            (Intuition)
                               INTU
                                12
                                 |
                                 |  7.8 WED
                                 |  6.3 NATL.
                                 |
                                 6
                                 |
                                 |
                                 |
                            WED  |  NATL.
 L    15 — 10 — 5 — 7.8 — 6.2 — 5 — 10 — 15   R
(Left)              (Integrative)            (Right)
                                 |
                                 |
                                 6
                                 |
                                 |
                                 |
                                12
                                 T
                            (Thinking)
```

TABLE 3.3 L-T Scale Score for Engineering and Administration Managers at WED

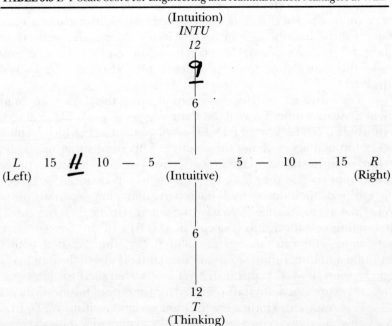

```
                            (Intuition)
                               INTU
                                12
                                 9
                                 +
                                 6
                                 |
                                 |
                                 |
 L    15  //  10 — 5 —    — 5 — 10 — 15   R
(Left)              (Intuitive)           (Right)
                                 |
                                 |
                                 6
                                 |
                                 |
                                 |
                                12
                                 T
                            (Thinking)
```

sex and occupational specialization will and should occur. But, the data also indicate some individual mismatches exist that may be targets for possible productivity improvement. For example, the Engineering and Administrative Divisions' management, on the average, tend to exhibit an L-T style which is characterized by a heavy reliance on facts, figures, and formal structure for making decisions. This would appear to be a style consistent with the functions carried out in this division where a premium is placed on accuracy, detail, and precision (for example, estimating and production scheduling). Hence, we can see that the managers working in this division appear to be working where their talents and preferences are best suited.

On the other hand, the BMS score results for some individual managers suggest that their management style does not match well with the divisional emphasis or particular duties they are expected to perform.

TABLE 3.4. Examples of Possible Mismatch Between Management Style and Position Held

DIVISION	MOST TYPICAL MANAGEMENT STYLE	LEAST TYPICAL MANAGEMENT STYLE
Engineering	L-T	R-INTU
	I-T	I-INTU
Administration	L-T	R-INTU
	I-T	I-INTU
Art production	I-INTU	L-T
	R-INTU	I-T
Creativity	I-INTU	L-T
	R-INTU	I-T

In these cases, care should be taken to review and assess the managers' actual performance, job satisfaction, and other factors for other indications of a possible mismatch. It could be that these individuals are quite competent, but simply misplaced within WED. Reassignment elsewhere could be a simple and very productive solution both for WED and the individuals concerned. Or, it could be that these individuals have been fully capable of being successful in their present positions even though they have *much greater potential* for success if they were placed elsewhere where their underlying capabilities could be more effectively used. Or, an overall assessment may reveal that there are people that should be considered for outplacement programs.

One piece of information that often helps to interpret the above scores is health statistics. Usually if there is a mismatch on the job, stress will be higher than average. Health problems could reveal the impact of the stress felt. You, as president, examine personnel files with this in mind only to uncover another important productivity opportunity. WED does not have a comprehensive health program in effect for management at this time. This concerns you since you anticipate that stress itself may be a major health hazard at WED—not to mention the importance of health statistics to assist you in making productive management decisions as noted above. You jot this down for further action in the future.

You turn to BMS scores to see if they can also be helpful to you for improving the communication within WED where conflict has erupted in the past. You find that the scores hold many clues. For example, you note that the average scores for the Engineering and Administrative Divisions are quite different from that of the Art Production and Creative Divisions (See Table 3.5). It appears that managers in the first two divisions emphasize styles of L-T or I-T while the latter two divisions tend to use I-INTU or R-INTU styles. In short, the management in each of these divisions tends to use widely different ways of approaching organizational problems. They simply see the world of management from a totally different perspective. Up to now, they have sought to convince each other that their method is the best way. Until they develop a better understanding of how each of their respective approaches is important to the fulfillment of overall WED goals, conflict will continue. (See Table 3.6.) This is another opportunity to increase productivity through such vehicles as training in such interpersonal skills as empathy and sensitivity. The pattern of BMS scores within each division can also be used to suggest which managers can best serve as facilitators for conflict resolution when it does occur.

You, as president of WED, have been aware that conflict has also occasionally erupted between men and women on the job, and you won-

TABLE 3.5. Dominant BMS Styles Used by WED Division

DIVISION	STYLES
Engineering	L-T
Administration	I-T
Art production	I-INTU
Creativity	R-INTU

TABLE 3.6. How Different Management Styles by Division Combine to Achieve Organizational Goals

Style	L-I I-T	+ R-INTU I-INTU	= I-INTU
Focus	Facts	+ Possibilities	= Facts and possibilities
Methods used	Practical and impersonal	+ Personal, insightful, and enthusiastic	= Personal, insightful, and practical
Divisions where found in WED	Engineering Administration	+ Production Creativity	= Effective total organizational team

der if the way each sex thinks and approaches his or her job is one factor that generates this conflict. BMS scores indicate that there are significant differences between the sexes on the average across the organization. (See Table 3.7.) Men tend to employ an L-T or I-T style more frequently, and women tend to use a R-INTU or I-INTU style. In short, men tend to rely more on facts and figures to make their management decisions while women tend to rely more on feelings.

TABLE 3.7. How Different Management Styles by Sex and/or Individual Combine to Achieve Organizational Goals

	MEN		WOMEN		WED
Most typical style	L-T I-T	+	R-INTU I-INTU	=	I-INTU
Focus	Facts	+	Feelings	=	Facts and feelings
Method used	Practical and impersonal	+	Personal, insightful, and enthusiastic	=	Personal, insightful, and practical

Again, both management styles are important to the overall effective functioning of WED. You conclude that productivity can also be enhanced if you institute training programs where each sex (and individual) can not only see and understand how each division in WED interfaces and contributes to the completion of organizational tasks, but also how each sex (and variation by individual) contributes as well.

One of the issues you had hoped a BMS assessment could help you with was selecting a team within WED best able to handle the task of identifying what the organization's goals should be over the next decade. You already know who the key division heads are, and you now have some picture of who the most productive managers have been and are likely to be based on a review of personnel records and the BMS assessments conducted above. But, just who from this group should serve on the future goals management team? Also, can this task be handled successfully from within or should you also employ an outside consultant?

As president, you are aware of the fact that practically any effort to identify future goals for WED will have to include your division heads and top potential managers if you hope to have these goals successfully implemented thereafter. But, you find that BMS assessments can be effectively used *to structure how* these managers will work most productively in carrying out this task.

For example, you know that the managers who have the highest R and INTU scores are the ones with the most creative potential. They are the managers most likely to come up with totally new and original ways to deal with the future of WED and to see the different possible ways to reorganize as appropriate. On the other hand, those managers with high L and T scores are most likely to be able to critically assess the new proposals and ideas that are surfaced and to practically implement them once an agreed agenda has been reached. You also know that R and INTU managers' capacity to generate new creative ideas is affected by the environment in which they work. They tend to be put off by too much direction before they have had a chance to give their own input. They also seem to function best in more informal settings, whereas the L and T style managers prefer more formal structure and step-by-step patterns of decision making.

You conclude that the best way to select and form your future goals team is to separate your key managers into two groups at first. Group 1 will be the R and INTU managers and Group 2 will be the L and T managers. (See Table 3.8.) You will give Group 1 the task of future goal generation and development. The instructions you give the group will be in sufficient detail to give general guidance and direction, but not so detailed as to thwart their sense of creativity.

TABLE 3.8. Using Management Styles to Identify WED's Future Goals

GROUPS	TEAM 1	TEAM 2	CONSULTANT
Most Typical Style	R-INTU	L-T	I-INTU
Capabilities	Sees possibilities Ingenious Can deal with complexities and imponderables	Sees facts Can analyze, organize, and find flaws	Can identify new ideas that can also be practically implemented. Is conciliatory and persuasive

Group 2 will be given the task of reviewing Group 1's input, identifying those goals and objectives that seem most plausible, and developing a plan for implementation that is realistic. You also assign who scored highest on the I scale. They will be most capable of being empathetic to the input of both groups of managers and also of understanding how to put the input together into a working functioning plan for action.

You also conclude that it is most desirable to hire an outside consultant to design and guide this overall future goal project. Although the present management team will carry the primary responsibility for both goal identification and later implementation, an outside consultant will be able to serve important functions that the existing management staff probably is not as capable of performing since they are so personally involved with the project emotionally. One key function is to ensure greater objectivity and openness to new concepts as well as help to ensure a balanced assessment of past performance issues. Another is to help guide the I managers in facilitating the effective interaction between the various brain and management styles in the two groups. This approach is most likely to encourage R and INTU managers' creative input at the outset. They will feel there is no evidence of a canned fixed agenda that must come out at the end of this process and, therefore, that their input is truly sought and valued. Similarly, L and T managers will recognize that their input is also valued since they will have ample opportunity to review and comment on the proposals that are surfaced as well as generate some of their own if necessary.

Other Practical Ways to Use BMS Assessments

The simulated exercise we just went through at WED should give you a good sense of some of the possible ways that BMS assessments can be used to manage organizations more productively.[9] Let's go through and review a few more selected applications now and show in more detail how some of the instruments mentioned above can be used to conduct in-depth BMS programs.

There are a wide variety of situations in organizations where an ability to measure right brain skills and locate the persons who possess them can be used practically to increase production. We know for example that persons who have the most creative ability tend to score higher on scales that measure intuition (INTU). Creative ability would be particularly valuable to perform such organizational tasks as marketing, buying for future trends, forecasting, and intelligence work—just to name a few examples.

TABLE 3.9. Practical Use of Intuition in Organizations

SKILLS POSSESSED	EXAMPLE OCCUPATIONS WHERE USEFUL
Sees possibilities	Marketing
Supplies ingenuity to problems	Intelligence
Can deal with and solve complex issues where data is incomplete	Buying
	Counseling
Furnishes new ideas	Writers
Sees the future	Sales
Motivates people to do the impossible	Nursing
	Personnel/Organizational development

Portions of this table have been adapted and reproduced by special permission of the publishers, Consulting Psychologists Press, Inc., Palo Alto, California 94306 from *Introduction to Type* by Isabel Briggs Myers, copyright © 1980. Further reproduction is prohibited without the publisher's consent.

Interestingly, organizations appear to do a better job of assessing and knowing where left brain skills and abilities are located in their organizations than where right brain skills, such as intuition, are located. Organizations also appear to spend little time assessing whether right brain skills are present in adequate quantity and developing to their full potential in order to help assure its future survival. As one illustration, ask a group of managers one day to name the number of chairs in the room you're sitting in. You will find everyone can agree on the correct answer. Then ask them to tell you what the creative potential is in the room. Not only will they not be able to give you the answer, they probably will have little idea about how to get a semblance of an answer.

BMS assessments can help you measure the creative potential in your organization. These assessments can also be used to locate the individuals who possess this ability and give you some indication as to whether the skill is being used on the job at present to the greatest degree possible. This information can, in turn, be used by you in a wide variety of practical ways to improve performance such as helping you assign the correct people to particular tasks, effective team building, and designing training programs.

Let's take one example of a well known projection technique called the *Delphi Technique.* Normally, what is done in this approach is to pool expert opinion about what the future will be and make projections based on the common consensus of the experts. William Asher and David Loye, experts in forecasting and future's work respectively, have pointed out that this technique for projecting the future can be made more accurate with some refinements.[10] Let us say you wish to get an assessment of how some future trends are likely to affect your organization and to identify ways management should go about dealing with these trends. One way to make this technique more accurate is to use BMS assessments to identify persons in your organization to be the Delphi projectors. Persons scoring high on instruments that measure intuitive ability (INTU) would be more likely to be accurate than a random selection of projectors or experts.

At least two instruments we have mentioned so far can be used to measure intuitive ability with varying degrees of refinement. The first instrument, Test Your Management Style, can be used to give you a quick picture of where intuitive ability is located in your organization, the degree it is possessed, and whether or not the person appears to be using the skill on the job very effectively. It can also be used to give you an indication of whether the person is presently working in a position where his or her intuitive ability is likely to be used productively. If your search requires greater refinement and precision, The Myers-Briggs Type Indicator will give you a much greater in-depth measurement for intuition as well as measures for other right and left brain skills. Here is how these instruments can be used for this purpose. As we outlined in Chapter 2, Test Your Management Style (TYMS) measures on a scale from 0 to 12 intuitive vs. thinking ability. Scores of 10 to 12 would be high on either side of the scale, scores of 6 to 8 would be above average, and 0 to 3 below average. The instrument also measures which brain skill is *actually* being used on the job to make decisions (left, right, or integrative). A score of 11 to 15 would be high, 0 to 5 low, and 6 to 10 in the middle of the scale. The *top score* on each part of the test when combined together make up your overall management style. (See Table 3.10.)

TABLE 3.10. TYMS Test Scoring

PART	WHAT IT MEASURES	TYPES	SCALE RANGE
I	Actual management style on the job	Left, right, and integrative	0 to 15
+ II	Potential ability	Intuition and thinking	0 to 12
Total test	Management type	Top scale score on each part of test	

If a person is working at his full potential, he should be *aligned*. That is, the person will be using a style on the job consistent with his/her underlying ability. Similarly, for the job to be a good match, it *also needs to be aligned.* That is, the position should require that the person is using his or her underlying potential ability on a regular basis to complete the tasks inherent in that position. Hence, good candidates for The Delphi Projection Project should score from 10 to 12 on the intuition scale of the test that measures potential ability. They should also be actually using either an R or I decision-making style on the job (see Table 3.11).

TABLE 3.11. TYMS Test Scores That Indicate Alignment

GOOD	POOR
R-INTU	L-INTU
I-INTU	R-T
L-T	
I-T	

Let's suppose that you locate 30 people in your organization who score from 10 to 12 on the intuition scale of the test, but only ten of these people are properly aligned. These ten would be your prime Delphi candidates (examples are cases 1 to 3 in Table 3.12). However, you need not permanently eliminate all the other potential candidates from future projects. The pattern of scores they obtained on the test can be useful information for you to use in the future on this project or to make other changes within your organization that can increase overall productivity.

TABLE 3.12. How to Use Scores on TYMS Test for Delphi Project Recruitment

SAMPLE OF POTENTIAL CANDIDATES						PERSONNEL ACTION	REASON SELECTED OR REJECTED
Number	Score Distribution						
	L	R	I	T	INTU		
1	0	15	0	2	10	Selected	High INTU, aligned
2	0	3	12	0	12	Selected	High INTU, aligned
3	3	9	3	1	11	Rejected	High INTU, aligned
4	9	3	3	4	11	Rejected	High INTU, but not aligned
5	8	3	4	7	5	Rejected	L-T style

For example, you may find that some of your potential candidates have very high intuitive ability, but appear to be using a style on the job that is not consistent with it (for example, candidate 4 in Table 3.12). This manager would appear to be a prime candidate for training programs that would help him or her get better in touch with his or her underlying intuitive ability as well as develop the capacity to rely on this skill to make decisions in a more productive way. At the same time, let's say that a pattern of test scores also suggests that some of your other potential candidates have high intuitive ability, but an analysis of the positions they are currently in indicate that they may well be mismatched. After further analysis and assessment, you may conclude that these managers would be more productive as well as more satisfied personally by reassignment elsewhere in the organization.

Let's say for a minute that the project you are recruiting for requires much more precision and in-depth measurement than the TYMS test can provide. Not only do you need an assessment of intuitive ability, but you would also like to have some indication of how managers who are intuitive in your organization can be more effectively motivated to produce, and how they can be best teamed with other management types to get organizational tasks accomplished most productively.

The Myers-Briggs Type Indicator (MBTI) can be used effectively to assist you. The MBTI taken as a whole gives you a snapshot picture of the left and right brain skills that you have in your organization just like the TYMS does. However, it gives you this information more precisely with much greater depth along more dimensions. Therefore, the test results

TABLE 3.13. Personality Dimensions Measured by MBTI

LEFT BRAIN $\rightarrow$	INTEGRATIVE $\leftarrow$	RIGHT BRAIN
	Scale Scores	
Maximum 60	*Minimum* 0	*Maximum* 60
Extraversion (E)_____		_____Intraversion (I)
Sensing (S) _____		_____Intuition (N)
Thinking (T) _____		_____Feeling (F)
Judging (J) _____		_____Perceptive (P)

Combinations make
up 16 management types

Adapted and reproduced by special permission of the publisher, Consulting Psychologists Press, Inc. from the *Myers Briggs Type Indicator Report Form* by Isabel Briggs Myers, copyright © 1976. Further reproduction is prohibited without the publisher's consent.

can be used even more productively to guide your human resource management decisions.

The brain styles from left to right that are measured by the MBTI consist of four distinct dimensions. The scale scores on each of these dimensions can be combined to make up 16 different management types in your organization.

How can this information be used practically? You now have an overall picture of where the brain skills are located in your organization, to what degree, and along separate dimensions. This gives you the necessary tools with the necessary precision to recruit and place your management staff to function most productively with the greatest personal satisfaction possible. For example, if you wish to construct a management team that will not only work well together on a personal basis, but will also possess the brain skills necessary to get organizational problems solved, the MBTI can help you in the process. Table 3.14 summarizes just along the intuitive-sensing dimension how opposite brain skills can be used to complement each other in management settings. Table 3.15 shows how when managers are combined along several of the MBTI dimensions, skills and preferences can potentially be put together to accomplish organizational goals most productive in a work setting.

Once identified, MBTI scores can also be used for clues about how to best motivate each management type to perform at its maximum capacity. David Keirsey and Marilyn Bates have written an excellent book entitled, *Please Understand Me: An Essay in Temperament Styles,* that describes in detail how to relate to each management type in this way. Take for example an ENFP. According to Keirsey and Bates, they make excellent salespeople, advertising executives, and screen or play writers.

People to people work is essential for them. ENFP's often find it difficult to work within constraints of an institution, especially in following rules, regu-

TABLE 3.14. Combining Managers to Complement Each Other

SKILLS AND PREFERENCES	
Ways Intuitive Managers Need Sensing Types	*Ways Sensing Managers Need Intuitive Types*
Bring up pertinent facts	Bring up new possibilities
Apply experience to problems	Supply ingenuity to problems
Notice what needs attention now	See how to prepare for the future
Have patience	Have enthusiasm
Keep track of essential details	Watch for new essentials
Face difficulties with realism	Tackle difficulties with zest

Portions of this table have been adapted and reproduced by special permission of the publisher, Consulting Psychologist Press, Inc., Palo Alto, California 94306 from *Introduction to Type* by Isabel Briggs Myers, copyright © 1980. Further reproduction is prohibited without the publisher's consent.

TABLE 3.15. Using MBTI Scores to Build Management Teams

LEFT BRAIN TYPES	→	INTEGRATED MANAGEMENT TEAM	←	RIGHT BRAIN TYPES	
Type	Skills		Skills		Type
E	Good at greeting people Communicate freely Act quickly		Careful with details Work well alone Think before acting		I
S	Reach conclusions step by step Seldom make factual errors Good at precision work		Reach quick conclusions Often makes factual errors Dislikes taking time for precision work		N
T	Analytical Cool Logical		Persuasive Conciliatory Warm		F
J	Like to get things settled and finished Judge quickly		Adaptive Likely to be empathetic		P

Portions of this table have been adapted and reproduced by special permission of the publisher, Consulting Psychologists Press, Inc., Palo Alto, California 94306 from *Introduction to Type* by Isabel Briggs Myers, copyright © 1980. Further reproduction is prohibited without the publisher's consent.

lations, and standard operating procedures. Variety in doing day-to-day operations and interactions best suits the talents of ENFP's, who used quite a bit of latitude in which to exercise their adaptive ingenuity.[11]

As suggested earlier, instruments like the MBTI can also be used to increase organizational productivity. This can be accomplished in a number of ways. One example is to use the MBTI in your overall job placement program. This can be done at the initial placement stage, or to assess if a person is properly placed at present. The MBTI can also be used to help design a career development program for your managers that will help increase long-term productivity as well as personal job satisfaction.

Recent research conducted on the use of the MBTI to place managers in the proper occupation consistent with their brain skills and management styles shows clearly that executives can be more effectively placed using this instrument as one guide. Table 3.16 shows how four personality types are distributed across selected occupational specialties. Clearly, sensing-thinking types (ST's) prefer the occupations of accounting and banking. As outlined in Table 3.16, this is not surprising since ST's prefer to focus their attention on facts and prefer to make decisions using impersonal analysis. Similarly, SF's prefer sales and customer relations occupations. Again, this is consistent with the personality profiles outlined in Table 3.16. Although SF's also focus their attention on facts, unlike ST's, they handle these facts with personal warmth. They tend to be sympathetic and friendly and to enjoy occupational settings where they can provide practical help and service to people.

TABLE 3.16. Dominant Brain Style by Occupational Specialization

OCCUPATION	MBTI BRAIN SCORE (%)			
	ST	SF	NF	NT
Accountants	64	23	4	9
Bankers	47	24	11	18
Sales customer relations	11	81	8	0
Creative writers	12	0	65	23
Research scientists	0	0	23	77
Finance and commerce	51	21	10	18
Counseling	6	9	76	9
Nursing	15	44	34	7
Health-related professions	13	36	44	7

Portions of this table have been adapted and reproduced by special permission of the publisher, Consulting Psychologists Press, Inc., Palo Alto, California 94306 from *Gifts Differing* by Isabel Briggs Myers, copyright © 1980. Further reproduction is prohibited without the publisher's consent.

Properly used, the MBTI can also be helpful in reducing turnover. In a pre-post test of a gas company, it was found that over a 9-year period, those employees most likely to leave (80%) were Thinking Types whereas 80% of the Feeling Types still remained on the job. Apparently, F types *feel* a greater sense of personal satisfaction and identification by being loyal to the same employer than the analytical impersonal types do.[12]

Assessment of the job assignment and brain skill pattern of present managers can also be helpful in guiding mergers, takeovers, and other reorganizational efforts that will be most beneficial both to the organizations, units, and managers most involved. Take this case study of 22 accountants in a utility company as one example. All were supervisory grade or higher. Only three of the group were intuitives, and *not one* of the three was satisfied or satisfactory where they were. In an effort to improve the situation, the executive type intuitive (ENTJ) was made assistant comptroller. This new position was more appropriate for the ENTJ because it demanded his existing skills for organization and design more than his personal accuracy with numbers and figures which was his weaker suit. Within 2 years, he was offered the position of Comptroller.[13] A recent bank merger illustrates the potential use of the MBTI in conducting BMS assessments even better.

An INTP whom the bank acquired through a merger seemed to be a misfit in every department where he was tried. No supervisor wanted to keep him. At last there was a vacancy in securities analysis, which the personnel department had been waiting for. The INTP was transferred there and has had top ratings ever since.[14]

There is significant evidence to indicate that the MBTI can be used effectively to transcend the boundaries of language and culture as well in management settings. This fact would appear to have practical relevance to the top management of General Motors Corporation and Toyota Corporation as they proceed on their joint venture to produce small cars in California by 1984, and to help overcome the differences in American and Japanese management attitudes that have already surfaced.[15]

The key opportunity that appears to exist in this merger situation is for the management of both companies *to learn how* to combine the advantages of the right brain inductive style of Japanese management with the left brain deductive style of the United States just as the imagineers and engineers at Walt Disney Enterprises *needed to learn* how they could work to complement each other in a productive way. When this can be achieved, synergy will become a reality, and productivity as well as job satisfaction will increase dramatically.

> When coworkers differ on both perception and judgement, they have a problem. Working together will teach them something valuable if they respect each other, but it can be disastrous if they do not. As a team, they have at their disposal skill in both kinds of perception and both kinds of judgment. They need to understand each other well enough to see the merit of the other's skills and to use them.[16]

The MBTI can be used as one instrument to help guide this process effectively. The Nippon Recruit Center in Tokyo has used a Japanese translation of the MBTI for many years to place workers in business and industry successfully. We also noted in Chapter 2 that our testing of executives nationally indicated that executives with Asian backgrounds on the average possessed a higher level of intuitive ability that appears to be linked to the way families in the Eastern world bring up their children (inductively) compared to the Western world (deductively). This information along with other test results and personnel data can be used to determine which overall management approach to use in this and other similar cross-cultural settings, and to develop the training materials necessary to implement such efforts.

One key difference between the way managers are brought up in this country as compared to Japan and some other countries is in the emphasis on competition versus cooperation on the job and in our personal lives. There is much evidence to indicate that increasingly managers even in the United States are taking a fresh look at the possible advantages of adopting a more cooperative management style in both the public and private sectors. As noted in Chapter 1, this will require a virtual revolution in attitudes—or what is commonly referred to as a change in consciousness. BMS assessment instruments such as the TYMS, MBTI, and other synergistic games and exercises mentioned earlier can be helpful in bringing this change in attitude about successfully.

The fact is that each brain style and/or personality type has, when standing alone, certain strengths and weaknesses. However, when managers learn to work cooperatively together as a team toward a common goal, blind spots in decision making can be better avoided, productivity increased, and job satisfaction improved enormously by creating an *esprit de corp* that lifts the spirit to new heights of creativity and imagination. In day-to-day management, what this means is that "we say what we mean and mean what we say." Put another way, future organizational settings will demand that managers not only seek input from their staff, but learn how to use it when they get it. It also means that professional managers and staff need to learn, understand (cognitively and affectively), and value the input received from sources both on the right and the left so that it can be *integrated* into an overall plan of action that is likely to be effective and implementable at the least possible cost. In a nutshell, managers need to learn better *how to* communicate and *be open* to communication.

William S. Howell notes that the typical CEO makes decisions intuitively and then calls in his/her data person to support the decision analytically.[17] It is clear from what we have presented here that some managers have outstanding ability to reach the correct (or an effective) decision intuitively. It is also clear that there are situational settings where this approach may be the most effective method to use. But, it is also true that one of the potential dangers for the intuitive manager is projection (incorrectly interpreting one's own wishes to be an accurate perception of reality or the future). One of the best ways to guard against the danger of developing blind spots (whether from the left or the right) is to learn *to listen* and *hear* input from other sources, and then integrate this input into the basis for your final decision. It is also one of the best ways of insuring that you are getting maximum input from your staff as well as yourself. Managers *who know* (cognitively and affectively) that their input is valued are more likely to give it.

Hughes Aircraft in California recently hired an outside consulting firm to assess the attitude of its employees to company policies and practices. Perhaps the most significant finding in the study was that the vast majority of the respondents *did not* believe that present patterns would change nor that their suggestions for change would ever be seriously considered for implementation.[18]

Carl Sagan puts it this way.

There is no way to tell whether the patterns extracted by the right hemisphere are real or imagined without subjecting them to left-hemisphere scrutiny. On the other hand, mere critical thinking, without creative and intuitive insights, without the search for new patterns, is sterile and doomed. To solve complex problems in changing circumstances requires the activity of both cerebral hemispheres.[19]

Management Games to Demonstrate the Power of BMS Assessments

Here is just one illustrative game you can play in your organizations to demonstrate the power of BMS assessments for increasing organizational productivity and job satisfaction. I recommend games like this because it tends to be a more comfortable way for executives to *understand* (both know cognitively and feel it affectively) *that which they already know to be true* but are often afraid to admit—for whatever reason.

Take a group of ten to 20 managers—preferably from *different* management levels. If possible, try to include a few managers who are in direct supervisor-subordinate relationships. Also try to include at least two representatives from each sex. You might also wish to include a few other factors such as large age differences. The factors you pick will depend on the particular personal or organizational problem you have at hand.

If this information is not already available in your organization, administer the MBTI test. Score the results and keep a record of each person's personality type and range on the various scale scores. Now take a game like Desert Survival developed by Human Synergistics Inc.[20] Divide your management group up into two teams. The *key now* is to load each team by MBTI type. You can load your groups in alternative ways depending on your goals. For our purposes here, let's load the groups so that one team is heavily weighted to the intuitive side of the scale while the other team is heavily weighted in the opposite direction on this same dimension (highly sensing or left brain oriented).

Now the game begins. Desert Survival consists of taking a list of items and prioritizing their importance from high to low for survival in the desert. First of all, *each participant* makes his *own* priority list without discussing how he reached his conclusions. Each list is recorded on a score form. Next, the two respective teams carry out the same exercise and reach a team consensus. Then this team score is also recorded. During both stages of the game, it is desirable to have a specific time limit and create an environment where each team and the individual members are free to choose how they will sit and interact.

Assuming that you are an OD staff or outside consultant for the organization in question, you give the game instructions, the time limits, and assess the final scores. Throughout the game, you also periodically eavesdrop on each team. Record where they are in the process of prioritizing the items on the desert survival list (how many have they agreed on?); at different time intervals record how the group and individuals interact, and other key items (for example, what style does each group work with to solve the problem?). But more importantly, at the end of the game your role is to interpret the results and share with each participant how his score on the MBTI (in this case, along the intuitive-sensing dimension) affected his score in the game, the style each team adopted to solve the game problem, and also how each individual interacted during the process. Since you have kept a detailed record, you can now give them live playback about how they interacted. A videotape playback would be particularly effective here.

Here is how you can do this. First of all, discuss and explain the MBTI test and what it measures. Next, explain in a manner that each manager can understand, without being personally exposed, what the results mean. One way to do this is to give abstract case examples by type or summarize your own type for them. This latter approach can be particularly effective since there is a tendency for managers to open up if you as leader show the way.

The next step is to explain how and why you loaded the group in the way you did. Here, it might be helpful to reinforce your purpose for doing so, and make clear how this will help to understand how and why they just played the game the way they did. Next describe how to score the game—both the individual scores and the team scores. Also explain that the game was created by a desert survival expert, and give some information on his credentials.

Now the real fun—and real work—begins. Invariably, each team constructed in the manner I outlined will have just worked on this problem differently, as will the individuals in the group. The style they use will normally be different, and the productivity of their work will also vary (as measured by their final score and rate of progress during the game). You can feedback this information to the participants in a variety of ways so that they will clearly *know* (mentally know and emotionally feel) the important practical use BMS assessments can have on their organization's and their own productivity and satisfaction.

Here are some suggested ways for doing so. As a general guide, periodically throw in a little humor along with what you are telling the participants. This will help them to swallow some sensitive revelations they will probably come to feel along the way. Also remember you have placed a few managers who are working "for" each other in the group, and using humor as a vehicle for assisting in expanding awareness can be just the right touch. Example jokes might be "Rise above principle to the politics of the matter" or "You know you are moving in the right direction the degree to which resistance increases." As for the factual part of this exercise, try to explain by specific examples how each group worked differently. For example, you might point out that the sensing group tends to break problems down into logical step-by-step chunks and approach the problem with a relatively more serious tone. The intuitive group, on the other hand, tends to be lighter in tone and style, and work at the problem in a variety of ways. (Seldom have I seen such a group go *in order* from item one to 15 as the sensing types usually do.)

You will also be able to feedback symbolic words, postures, and positions each person took. The important point to make all along the way is how BMS styles *affect the results!* Urge the group to focus on such questions as: Were we productive? How could we be more so? What did the other group do that we can learn from? Try to move the discussion to an individual level of awareness at this point. For example, you might be able to effectively show how the two teams could complement each other and do still better—and then play another game to show them so right on the spot! Or you might feedback what one or two managers said or did at key junctures in the game and the impact it had on the final scores. You might also spend some time discussing how each person could work more effectively to support each other and the group in the future—such as in the next game or at work.

It would be particularly effective at this point for you to move the group on to an actual live problem they face at work—or take a series of them that *the group itself* has selected for examination. Usually at this point managers are ready to "bite into a real apple" (especially if you are working with Apple Computer managers!) This might also be a good time to move to the introduction of techniques, such as meditation, that will help them to tap into and expand their right brain skills, such as intuition.

In Chapter 4, we will analyze and describe now step-by-step methods in which the right brain skill intuition can be effectively developed and integrated with left brain skills to make effective management decisions. We will then go on in Chapter 5 to examine some of the most cutting-edge applications of the use of intuition in management and government today.

4

How to Develop and
Use Your Intuition
in Management

We started this book by saying that today most management training programs, whether presented in formal academic settings or within organizations, emphasize left brain analytical techniques for making management decisions. We have pointed out, however, that right brain skills such as intuition *are also* important resources for decision making. Indeed, we contend that there are certain settings and situations where the use of intuition is either more useful or the only available basis on which to make decisions (for example, in top management, crises, rapid change, and where data are limited).

We have also presented research results to back up our argument based on field testing of over 2000 managers across the country in a wide variety of organizational settings in both the public and private sectors. Among our most significant findings is the fact that top executives appear to use a management style quite different from their subordinates. Top executives are characterized by a I-INTU style. That is, their key decisions are guided by intuition, but they also have the capacity to take input from sources on the left (facts) and on the right (feelings) and integrate it into an overall program that can be implemented effectively.

It is our contention that intuition is an important management skill that can be used to increase personal and organizational productivity. Through management testing, we have found that this skill varies significantly by management level, sex, occupational specialization, and ethnic background just as left brain skills and capabilities do. It is also our contention that organizations can sharply increase productivity by learning to use *all the brain skills* existing within an organization—whether from the left, right, or integrated. We advocate establishing brain skill/

management style programs, which should include training programs for the development and actual use of these skills in organizational settings, as one of the best vehicles for accomplishing this. In Chapter 3, we outlined in detail several ways that BMS programs can be used effectively to increase both productivity and job satisfaction.

In this chapter, we will outline step by step just how the right brain skill intuition can be developed so that it can *be relied on* to make management decisions. We will also show how intuition can be integrated with left brain sources of information to arrive at decisions that are the best in the context of the options currently available, and to generate new options not yet perceived as available. By doing this, it is our hope that managers will learn that *they can* rely on input from both the right and the left—*internally within themselves, within their organizations, and in their relationships with other parts of the world.*

HOW TO DEVELOP YOUR INTUITION

Basically, we all have some intuitive ability at birth. Some of us appear to have more than others—some of us may even be classified as "psychic." Some of us learn to get in touch with this ability, learn how to use the skill most effectively (what medium and under what circumstances), and even learn how to expand our skills further. On the other hand, some of us, for whatever reason, (family upbringing and/or life experiences) never do any of these things throughout our lifetime. In fact, some of us may even go so far as to emotionally block the intuitive ability we do have and, thereby, seldom or never use our existing ability to its full potential. There are many managers operating in organizations today far below their right brain potential. If they could learn how to get in touch with their ability, the managers, personally and the organization they work for, would profit enormously.

Sigmund Freud once said, "The mind is like an iceberg. It floats with one-seventh of its bulk above the water."[1] So it is with our intuitive ability. Just how do you go about getting in touch with your intuitive ability, develop it further, and learn to apply it in practical work settings? Basically, any program to develop intuition (whether a personal or organizational effort) should consist of at least these three basic components that address your cognitive, affective, and evaluational attitude about using this skill:[2]

- Methods to help you allow intuition to work.
- Methods to help you believe in it.
- Methods to help you cultivate and practice it.

Methods to Help You Allow Intuition to Work

There are a number of techniques that are useful to help you allow intuition to work for you in management. First, it is important to learn *cognitively* who you are. This means getting in touch with the level and type of intuitive ability you have and becoming fully aware of the kinds of skills and tasks you can and like to perform. How much you wish to learn about yourself in this regard will determine the tools you use to explore yourself with and also govern just how far you are likely to go in developing your intuitive ability.

Broadly speaking, managers who have a high level of intuitive ability tend to have a set of characteristics. Charles A. Garfield, a psychology professor at The University of California at San Francisco Medical School and head of the Peak Performance Center in Berkeley, has studied more than 1200 peak performers in various professions during the last 15 years to distill the key elements they have in common. His findings neatly parallel the common characteristics of highly intuitive managers.[3] (See Table 4.1.)

TABLE 4.1. Characteristics of Highly Intuitive Managers

Good self-image	Prefer informal to formal style
Curious	Focus on solutions rather than problems
Independent	Do not try to be all things to all people
Inner vs. Outer direction	
Prefer action to inaction	
Take risks	

Intuitive managers are particularly good at performing certain kinds of tasks and functions, but they are also characterized by having the potential for certain blind spots or perspectives which need to be watched for. Table 4.2 summarizes these aspects of an intuitive manager's personality.

Beyond these broad characteristics, not all intuitive managers are alike or get their intuitive insights in the same way. As noted in Chapter 1, managers also use their intuition to serve different roles and functions depending on the individual and situation involved. More specifically, intuitive managers can be further classified in terms of extroversion and introversion (Senate majority leader Howard Baker is an example of an extroverted intuitive and Albert Einstein is an example of an introverted intuitive), and also in terms of the medium in which they function most effectively. Some work well in public settings in cooperation with other managers, while others work best primarily alone in more isolated settings. Table 4.3 summarizes their respective management style.

TABLE 4.2. Capabilities of Intuitive Managers

SKILLS AND TASKS THEY CAN PERFORM	TENDENCIES TO WATCH FOR
Bring up new possibilities	Impatient with routine, details, or repetition
Supply ingenuity to problems	
Read signs of coming change	May reach conclusions too quickly and ignore some relevant facts
See how to prepare for the future	
Have enthusiasm	May follow inspiration even when clearly bad
Watch for new essentials	
Tackle difficulties with zest	Frequently make errors of fact
	Work in bursts of energy rather than the same rate each day
	Dislike precision details

Portions of this table have been adapted and reproduced by special permission of the publisher, Consulting Psychologists Press, Inc., Palo Alto, California 94306 from *Introduction to Type* by Isabel Briggs Myers, copyright © 1980. Further reproduction is prohibited without the publisher's consent.

TABLE 4.3. Management Style of Extroverted and Introverted Intuitive Managers

EXTROVERTED INTUITIVE	INTROVERTED INTUITIVE
Express self naturally and easily, works easily with others	Find self-expression difficult, prefer to work more alone
Most effective in the promotion and initiation of new enterprises	Most effective in promoting understanding and interpreting life experiences
Use inner awareness to understand how to approach a situation	Use a situation to get better inner understanding
Enthusiastic at outset, but sometimes fails to follow through on activities or details	Have difficulty persuading others to see clear answers or to implement them practically
Insight comes through personal interaction and/or touch	Insight comes through mental processes

Portions of this table have been adapted and reproduced by special permission of the publisher, Consulting Psychologists Press, Inc., Palo Alto, California 94306 from *Gifts Differing* by Isabel Briggs Myers, copyright © 1980. Further reproduction is prohibited without the publisher's consent.

Intuitive managers also differ according to the most effective medium by which their insights come to them. Some work best when they can touch a person or object before making a decision. Such executives are famous for insisting on a personal interview in such cases. Politicians such as former President Lyndon Baines Johnson are typical in this regard. Other managers work best mentally. They get their insight in isolation totally divorced from the stimulation of other people or outside objects. Jonas Salk, the inventor of the polio vaccine, is a good example here.

One of the best ways to get in touch cognitively with how much intuitive ability you have is to take one of the tests available that can measure it. For a quick general picture, use the TYMS test described earlier in the book. This instrument will tell you whether you score very high or very low in intuitive ability, and whether it is your strongest resource for making decisions as compared to relying primarily on facts to do so. The test will also give you a picture of whether or not you *actually* appear to be using your intuitive ability for making on the job decisions. So, you will have some sense whether or not you are working in the most productive manner *vis-à-vis* your underlying ability or whether you appear to be pushing water upstream instead. You can also use the test results to compare yourself with your coworkers and/or get a picture of the creative potential existing within your organization. The higher the score on intuition, the greater the creative potential is within your organization.

If you wish to learn not only how much intuitive ability you have but also what type of intuitive manager you are, the MBTI outlined in Chapter 3 will give you a good reading. From the test scores, you will be able to determine the level of intuitive ability you have in much greater depth than the TYMS told you. In addition, you will be able to learn whether and to what degree you are an extrovert or introvert intuitive. Finally, you will also be able to get a measure of other aspects of your personality (for example, whether you are extremely judgmental) that can affect your capacity to use the intuitive ability you have to make on the job decisions.[4]

Getting in touch with your intuitive ability in this manner can be one powerful way of putting it to use not only for yourself but also for your organization. Two executives (one from the public sector and the other from the private sector) put it this way after having the experience:

> I now believe that this focus . . . is extremely important in improving one's ability to manage people, not the least of which is oneself . . . extensive effort must be devoted to developing and teaching the techniques of application to managers and would-be managers.[5]
>
> I would like further information on the availability of the two tests taken . . . and to discuss with you in greater depth what the potential would be for a company such as ours to use these skills.[6]

Should you wish to go still further and explore your other psychic skills such as precognition (ability to see the future), the Mobius Psi-Q I and II Test instruments outlined in Chapter 3 are available for use. Alan Vaughan, the author of the book, *The Edge of Tomorrow: How to Foresee and Fulfill Your Future,* has also developed a software computer game for use with the Apple micro computer that measures your precognitive ability as opposed to chance scores.[7]

Besides these tests, begin to examine the process and means by which intuitive insights come to you. There are several ways to do this.

One is to begin to keep a systematic record of your insights in a journal. Include such information as how and when they come, by what means (for example, dreams), and keep a record of their accuracy. Doing this will help you to get a better understanding of how you function best. It will also give you a record to discuss with other professionally trained people to help you develop your ability further. This record will also give you an overall picture showing whether you in fact seek to implement the intuitive insights you receive or whether you have adopted the style of simply ignoring them. It will also give you clues as to how you might actually be blocking your intuitive ability from coming through to serve you.

Another way to help get in touch with your intuitive ability is *to share* your experience with others—whether it be friends, family members, or coworkers. Simply taking the risk of sharing the experiences you are having with others is a useful tool for unlocking this ability and developing it further. Psychologists will tell you that a pattern that recurs over and over in therapy is that the patient is afraid to share their experiences—whether good or bad—because they believe they alone are having them. One of the keys to solving personal problems—or to unlocking new doors—is to recognize this and share the experience with others. This sharing can be accomplished on a formal or informal basis. One step you might find helpful is to form a group of peers and/or friends that meets regularly to share intuitive experiences and work to develop them further. You might even take a problem you are trying to solve at work or in your personal life as a group project and make it the central concern of your intuitive work group for resolution. This experience will not only serve to give you support, it will help to teach you new ways of getting in touch with your intuitive ability. Another approach might be to have a regular time with your family in which each member can share his own experiences—such as sharing dreams from the night before at breakfast time.

Reading about the experiences of others who have gone before you in this field is another safe way to learn about yourself. You will be surprised to find that what is happening to you has already happened to others many times. You will also learn to profit from their experiences— to find other ways to recognize and tap into your ability, and learn to apply it day to day to help guide your decisions. Recent research has shown, for example, that one of the major obstacles to developing psychic ability among children is the fact that neither they, their teachers, or their parents understood or knew how to handle the process when it was unfolding.[8] Recently, medical research among schizophrenics has indicated that not all were ill. Instead some were gifted psychics whose intuitive insights were not understood by the world around them, rather than the other way around.[9]

An important way that organizations *can learn to benefit* from the potential intuitive ability of their managers is to create a personal/ organizational environment in which these skills are supported, valued, and practiced in day-to-day life to make decisions. Frequently, we reject new and different ways of solving problems because we become accustomed to a particular way of doing things. Often, it is only in a crisis (business failure, loss of health or loved ones) that we reach for alternative ways of doing things or allow our inherent intuitive skills to surface and be of assistance to us. As Woody Allen says, "If you're not failing every now and again, it's a sign you're not being very innovative in what you're doing." Put another way, making mistakes simply means you are learning faster.

Essentially, it is a productivity question. Organizations and the managers that lead them can use the right brain skill intuition to increase productivity by simply *allowing it to happen.* Roger Von Oech, president of Creative Think in Menlo Park, California, talks of it this way:

> I think the most important motive for coming up with new ideas is fun. Creative thinking is a lot of fun. I like to think of creative thinking as the sex of your mental lives.[10]

Ed Everett, an assistant county manager in Nevada, talks about the practical benefit that organizations can derive by allowing intuitive skills to function effectively:

> With shrinking revenues and demands to maintain service levels, why should you, as a manager, devote time, effort, or money to something as esoteric as creativity? For many organizations the human mind and the creative potential of the employee are one of the few remaining resources which can still be expanded. Not using this resource is the same as turning your back on a new revenue source.[11]

Besides recognizing and accepting that intuitive ability can be used to increase organizational productivity, it is important to *eliminate the interference that interrupts its flow.* This means tension, anxiety, fear, desire, or other similar blocks. *One's own mental attitude* is important. You must have a relaxed positive attitude about letting it happen. Research shows clearly that those people who feel they are creative are, while those who are not felt they were not. Van Oech has identified seven mental locks that managers impose on themselves and others that work to interrupt realizing their own and their organization's full creative potential: everything is fine, follow the rules, to err is wrong, playing is frivolous, that's not my area, be practical, and I'm not creative.[12] One manager describes what his personnel learned by working with exercises to expand their mental capital.

> We learned most by examining our inabilities to solve certain problems, a process that gave us insight on what each of us does to block creative solutions. Defining the problem too narrowly, making unnecessary assumptions that restrict thinking, and assuming all problems should be solved using only our left brain were some of the blocks we discovered.[13]

There are a wide variety of tools and techniques that can be used both on a personal and organizational level to help unblock our intuitive ability. Among those that have been used effectively in various settings in both the eastern and western world are hypnosis, meditation, guided imagery, dream analysis, and related holistic health applications such as diet and lifestyles analysis (for example, stress and biofeedback). The pattern of office design, seating, colors, music, and interpersonal communication can also play a very important part in facilitating the flow of right brain input to solve organizational problems.

More specifically, these techniques have been used practically in the following ways depending on the organization and problem at hand. Where appropriate, functioning with a very open, flexible technique or no meeting agenda has proved to be a means by which intuitive input is encouraged. Another useful technique is to segment meetings into creative open times rather than structured times. During these open periods, evaluation of proposed ideas (particularly by left brain managers) is held in abeyance. Experience has shown that these techniques are productive because intuitive managers tend to prefer being given a problem to solve, but resent being told *how to* solve it.

Creating a relaxed, informal, fun-type tone is also helpful. Intuitive types tend to prefer this method of addressing problems over a highly structured work format or methodology. Informal clothing and seating patterns is also normally preferred. Musical backgrounds including the use of formal meditation exercises before beginning to work on a specific problem also appears to facilitate generating creative input. Intuitive managers often prefer a warm environment in which to work—both in terms of colors and interpersonal communication. They appear to function best when they *feel* their input is truly solicited and given careful consideration. This is particularly so when totally new problems are being addressed where standard operating procedures have not yet been established. Emphasis on cooperative vs. competitive ways of solving problems appears to generate the most right brain input possible.

One highly successful company that regularly uses these techniques is Hawthorne/Stone, a San Francisco real estate firm. The founders of the company became millionaires in three years. Six of the firm's 34 staff members each earn over $200,000 per year. Marshall Thurber, William F. Raymond, and Rob Cassil, founders of the firm explain, "The true purpose of our real estate company is to create and play games together, transcending the economic limitations in a satisfying environment." Thurber goes on saying, "I felt that if I could set up an organization that comes from choosing to play rather than having to work to make a living, then we could create miracles."[14] There are no regular hours for the staff at H/S. The office decor is warm and homey. One of the staff tells about how she felt when she was hired. "When I came for my first interview, everyone was very positive, very friendly, very interested in who I was and where I was coming from."[15]

Methods to Help You Believe in Intuition

The pioneering research of Douglas Dean and John Mihalasky, authors of the book *Executive ESP,* showed that executives who scored highest on ability to use ESP and had the highest profit record also had one other important characteristic—*they believed in ESP!*[16] Mentally, how we think and what we are willing to accept or entertain as possible has an effect on what is possible. *We create our own reality!* Another term for this process is *negative power*—when we narrow the range of possible options simply by what we are willing to entertain as possible.

Frances Vaughan, the psychologist and author of the book, *Awakening Intuition,* found that many of her adult patients felt they were more intuitive as children, and that they learned to keep their intuitive perceptions to themselves after encountering skepticism or ridicule from adults.[17] What you need to learn to do is keep an open mind about the possibility that intuitive experiences are within your grasp and that your ability can be expanded further. As Jean Piaget, author and child psychologist says, "If you want to be creative, stay in part a child with the creativity and invention that characterize children before they are deformed by adult society."[18]

Laurence R. Sprecher, Senior Associate of Public Management Associates in Beaverton, Oregon, notes that people often presume a vast gap exists between logic and intuition. He asks:

> What if intuitive thinking was merely a subspecies of logical thinking—one in which the steps of the process were hidden in the subconscious portions of the brain? What if intuition was in reality a series of subconscious programs stored in the cerebrum and passed on from generation to generation? We know that, in other species, important information like migration patterns and survival reactions is passed on genetically. If we accepted the intuitive as an extension of the logical, wouldn't we be more comfortable using it? By treating intuition as something mysterious . . . do we not make it more difficult for most managers . . . to use it?[19]

Sprecher argues what is needed is an application of administrative androgeny that would allow us all to be both rational and intuitive, cognitive and emotional, competitive and nurturing—depending on what is appropriate for the situation at hand.

Examine your emotional state. Research shows that tension and anxiety interfere with learning of any kind. Examine your existing attitudes and beliefs about intuition. Become conscious of the fact that your own thoughts can work to create your own state of consciousness—learn to take responsibility for that! Suspend judgment for a moment—particularly if you scored high on being judgmental on the MBTI or high on express control (EC) on the FIRO-B instruments mentioned earlier. Entertain at least the possibility that intuition exists as a skill that you can use to make decisions on the job. Learn to listen to yourself—and to others. Well developed intuition is a clear and accurate perception of reality, both inner and outer. In order to get clear perception of reality, you must learn to distinguish between yourself (ego) and reality. Often when we become too ego-involved with a situation or person, we project. This is the unconscious process whereby we see in another person something we do not wish to acknowledge or accept in ourselves—either positively or negatively.

> The potentials of the mind are awesome. Sometimes one feels lazy, frightened, and uncertain in the quest for self-knowledge. Sometimes it seems easier to play old games, to maintain old images, unsatisfactory as they may be, than to risk stripping away the facade and seeing who one really is. Because of this, the commitment to awakening intuition requires relentless courage and a continuing willingness to face the unknown.[20]

I am reminded of experiences I have had on military bases across the country where I have trained officers in management skills. One of the exercises I have used to help increase participants' awareness of each other's skills and abilities including intuition is the synergistic game called Desert Survival produced by Human Synergistics in Plymouth, Michigan.[21] The purpose of the game is to show how individuals working together openly in a synergistic manner will result in better organizational decisions. The way the game works is that you are given a list of 20 objects and told to prioritize them in the order you would discard them so that you could survive on the desert. First, each individual works on the exercise alone and makes their choices. Then teams are formed, group decisions made, and then the scores compared for each individual and each team. Invariably, the group scores are better than the individual scores as a whole. But, certain individuals can score higher than the group did—or they come closest on an individual basis to beating the group score. They are called the key resource persons in each group.

The power of previous learning and conditioning to thwart the use of intuition in this exercise is amazing. Frequently, I find that female officers in the group *with no formal desert survival training at all* achieve the highest scores on the exercise—they have an intuitive sense of how to survive. You will note that this is consistent with our own national testing which showed that women managers on the average scored higher than men did. But, several factors often function to prevent women or other key resource people from using their intuitive knowledge to improve the decision of the total group. One factor is their own reluctance or inability to argue their case. Frequently, this is due to the fact that women are conditioned (or have allowed themselves to be conditioned) to take on more passive roles. In this case, women will often automatically adopt or willingly accept instructions to serve as recorder or secretary of the group rather than the role of a more active participant. On the other hand, male officers are more likely to try to take command of the group and seek to lead it—particularly if they have had desert survival training. It is significant to note that they often *are not* the key resource person in the group. They, more than anyone, are amazed when they find out *who is,* because it is often the person *they totally discounted*—and also the person that *discounted themselves!*

The moral of the story is that one of the keys to unlocking intuitive ability is our own mind set about the subject itself, and the role we assign to it and ourselves in making decisions in our lives. Communication is in part a relationship between the sender and the receiver. What we each believe to be so will affect what is so. Following the completion of this game, both the senders and the receivers in the group normally have had their awareness level so altered and expanded that they will never again be able to function at the same consciousness level as in the past.

Learning to believe in your intuitive ability, and that of others, means learning to take the basic steps outlined in Table 4.4.

TABLE 4.4. Steps to Learning About Your Intuitive Ability

STEP	*METHOD TO USE*	*EXERCISES TO PRACTICE*
1. *Quiet the mind*	Learn to relax. Don't try too hard. Develop sense of alert awareness.	Any form of meditation, open focus.
2. *Concentrate*	Focus your attention, visualize your mind as a lazer beam.	Self-hypnosis tapes, word association and problem-solving exercises.
3. *Be receptive*	Suspend judgment, be aware of yourself physically, mentally, and emotionally; listen to yourself and others accurately by holding ego in abeyance and avoiding projection.	Exercises such as "Who Am I?", "Who Are You?", and "What Does Our Organization Stand For?"

There are numerous exercises that you can try on a personal basis or in your organization to help you learn to believe in intuition. I will share a few with you here and refer you to the bibliography in the back of the book for other suggestions. One that I have found effective in workshop settings is to hand out a brief questionnaire where only the participants see their responses. It is an exercise designed to get them in a space where they will dialogue with themselves. It is designed to help them observe themselves without deception so that they can be honest with themselves. By focusing their attention on their responses to the questionnaire, it helps them to stop, take a moment in their active lives (perhaps the first time they have done so in years), and to focus their minds. The process gets them in touch with their intuitive ability. *They learn to know what they already know!*

The stage is first set by taking a brief break from the normal workshop activities. When the participants return, they are instructed to relax and get in a comfortable position. A meditation tape, including music, is played, and then the questionnaire is distributed. Each participant is told that he is free to share or not to share his responses with the other workshop participants as he wishes. Then begins the self-dialogue exercise. I ask these ten basic questions.

Self Dialogue Exercise

1. *I believe on faith in ESP.*
   (a) True
   (b) False
2. *I have had psychic experiences.*
   (a) Yes
   (b) No
3. *I have had occasions when I saw what was going to happen before it actually did happen.*
   (a) Yes
   (b) No
   If yes, describe the one you remember the most.
4. *Have you had a major trauma in your life in the last five years* (illness, lost a key job, got a divorce, lost a loved one, etc.)?
   (a) Yes
   (b) No
   If yes, what do you remember about your feelings *the day* you felt the worst?
5. *Have you had an idea recently at work (in the last year) that you feel is good for your organization, proposed it, but failed thus far to get it implemented?*
   (a) Yes
   (b) No
   If yes, list *one to three* examples *most* important to you.
6. *Do you like your present job?*
   (a) Yes
   (b) No
   Why? (Be specific.)

7. *Do you like the organization you are presently working for?*
   (a) Yes
   (b) No
   Why? (Be specific.)
8. *Are you really happy with the person you are living with? Or, if you are not living with anyone, are you happy about it?*
   (a) Yes
   (b) No
   Why? (Be specific.)
9. *If the answer is no, what does that tell you about yourself? (In each of all of questions 6 to 8).*
10. *Write down whatever is on your mind right now!*

There is no question that such an exercise has tremendous power. Participants during or after the workshop will come up and relate insights that have come to them ranging all the way from business problems to their own personal lives. The energy in the room in that moment is unmistakably higher. They have tapped into an energy source they had not been fully aware of before. A president of one large west coast firm wrote, "I applaud your work and hope you will continue to pursue it."[22] Another southwestern insurance partner with John Hancock later said, "Your recent seminar was excellent, and the thought occurred to me that you might be of some help to us in our agency."[23] Typical comments on evaluation forms later were, "I answered questions about myself that I was afraid to ask"; "The seminar helped me to see my potential and realize ways to develop it"; and "The seminar is a new beginning for the advancement of business."[24]

Imagery in various forms is another way to tap into your intuition. It can be exercised on several different levels:

- Affective—use dreams, fantasy, imagination as tools.
- Auditory—sounds, music.
- Kinesthetic—body movement, dance.
- Olfactory—smell.

One exercise you may wish to practice here is word concentration. Ask managers to simply reflect on what the word *intuition* means to them. Another technique is to sit across from a fellow manager you do not know. Imagine that this person is an animal. Describe the characteristics you see. Reverse the process and exchange with your partner, members of the group, and then seek the input of members who know this manager well. You will be amazed how accurate your perceptions are.

Practice similar exercises in an organizational context to get a sense of how intuitive insights can be practically applied to make management decisions. For example, start a business meeting differently than usual. Ask your staff to relax and sit in a comfortable position. Ask them to close their eyes and to imagine that they are surrounded by a warm white light. Ask them to think warmly of the things they like about their co-staff members, their job, and organization. Then ask them to slowly focus again to the present moment and ask them to try to solve a particular problem you are facing in the organization at that moment. Michael Ray and Rochelle Myers, professors at Stanford University Business School, are experimentally using such techniques at their classes there. One business student related after the experience, "It was one of the most valuable courses I have taken here. I hope the skills I learned in the course will stay with me for the rest of my life."[25]

Methods to Help You Practice Intuition

The third major step to take in developing your intuition is to cultivate and practice it daily. *Practice makes perfect!* Learn to take the risk of using your intuition to make decisions and learn from the process. Seek outside verification and then learn from your mistakes. Hone your ability to the point that you can clearly distinguish between your own ego and reality. We all possess the ability to use intuition to make decisions. Frequently, the primary reason we fail to develop our ability to the fullest is that we are simply lazy. It is analogous to the blind person who develops his or her other inherent senses to the point that color can be seen through touch. If a blind person can develop his or her other senses to this degree, why can't we develop our intuitive ability in the same way?

Frequently, we fail to make full use of our intuitive ability because we are afraid to give up methods of making decisions that we are used to or comfortable with—whether they are really effective or not. Getting in touch with and using your intuition may mean that you have to learn to *take the risk* of giving up old ways of thinking and doing things—in a word, *changing.*

> Imagination is the vehicle whereby intuition finds expression in life. Many of the constraints and limitations in one's life can be attributed to lack of imagination.[26]

Intuition does not evaluate. It indicates possibilities and provides insight into the nature of things. Ask yourself how many times you have had an inspiration or insight on how to solve a problem and then failed to follow up on it? Are you aware of how you close off the possible use of your intuition—and that of others in your organization?

Arthur Hastings, parapsychologist and management consultant, helps businessmen do this in workshops and on-sight settings by getting them to first learn to relax more by employing some of the techniques we have already discussed. He finds that creative solutions to problems that have been elusive come into focus.[27] Try this exercise yourself. Take a problem that is facing you in your organization or personal life that has you preoccupied. Work on defining the problem as clearly as possible. Even go so far as to write it down. Now, go through some of the steps outlined earlier that were used in workshops before the Dialogue with Self questionnaire was answered. Relax by playing soft music, travel your body from head to foot slowly relaxing the tension you feel anywhere at all. Once you are completely relaxed, imagine that you are in the woods. It is a warm sunny day. You can hear the wind rustling in the trees. You can hear a bird chirp here or there, and water is slowly rolling down a hill over rocks in a stream. You are sitting on the front porch of your lodge. You feel comfortable, strong, and at peace in this moment. You look out over the valley and see the sun reflecting against the mountains in the background. Your mind again turns to the problem that preoccupies you. . . . The solutions are coming to you now, and you see clearly what your next step should be.

Here are some steps to take in practicing the use of your intuition. Keep an idea journal. Whenever a flash of insight comes to you, write it down. This usually happens at times when you are in some sort of relaxed state such as after awakening from a dream, driving across the desert, watching the sun go down at night, or showering in the morning. Reflect on how you process the insight. Are you receptive, do you cut it off, ignore it, or follow up on implementing it? Reflect on key turning points in your life. What did you rely on then to make your key decisions? Was it only facts or were there important intuitive feelings involved? When a problem is concerning you, learn to sleep on it. Say to yourself, "I will put this problem to rest. I will sleep on it, and it will be solved in the morning." Keep a record of the decisions you make based on intuition. Be objective, and evaluate how often you are right or wrong. Analyze from time to time the ingredients that were involved *within yourself* in each case, and learn to eliminate or reduce the causes for error. Each day, consume a philosophical food whether it be a meditation tape, a book on Zen, a conversation about universal knowledge, or a weekend retreat to sit alone in the woods.

Perhaps a personal illustration from my own work will help clarify the importance of daily practice. The response form you completed earlier I send to every manager I test. On that form, I not only score the two parts of the TYMS test which measures both brain and management styles, but I also write in long hand whatever comes to me about the person at that time. Frequently, I will write whole paragraphs and get quite specific about patterns of behavior they exhibit and steps that they need to take in their management or personal lives. I follow the same practice in workshops, except that rather than writing down my perceptions on a response form, I give feedback that I receive verbally. I have found that personal hand touch will also give me impressions or pictures about the

individual. Usually, I will express whatever comes to me at the moment
and then seek verification for accuracy.

The results are sometimes amazing. Recently, I received this letter
from the wife of a CEO who herself is a president of a public relations and
marketing firm.

> Just a few minutes ago, my husband shared with me the results of the
> management style test which you mailed to him recently. Needless to say, I
> was so impressed with your comments that I decided to follow up with you
> for two reasons:
> - Would it be possible to mail me a questionnaire or test so that I may
>   complete it accordingly?
> - Considering the results of Pantin's test, which are surprisingly ac-
>   curate, do you recommend or suggest any existing publications or
>   management tool that could help someone develop existing
>   capabilities to the fullest?[28]

Another respondent wrote, "I want to tell you how much I appreciated
your letter last spring with the analysis of my management style. I must say
you were very accurate in the between-the-lines vibrations you picked up
about me."[29] Now, this does not mean that I am always on target about
everyone I practice this technique with (anymore than data-based decision making is 100% accurate all the time), and some people are easier to
pick up cues from than others. But, I am learning to be more accurate day
by day with practice, and as others become more open with me in workshops, we find that intuition can be used as one effective guide for making
decisions.

Case Examples of Organizations and Individuals Using Intuition to Increase Productivity

There are a number of ways that you and your organization can make the
use of intuition an integral part of day-to-day decision making. Practiced
regularly, it will serve you as a reliable resource. Joseph McKinney,
chairman and CEO of Tyler Corporation in Dallas, Texas, uses a technique called "the stray bullet drill." "When everything is going great, we
try to imagine what combination of circumstances could constitute a
serious threat to us."[30] Before McKinney begins this exercise, they start
each staff meeting on Monday with prayer—one form of meditation.
Their approach there is to try to tap into the spiritual level of intuition
described in Chapter 1. In essence, what they do is acknowledge that there
is a higher source of energy than themselves—in this case, God. McKinney
says, "We recognize in that prayer that we can't do anything without God's
help, and we also take great confidence from the knowledge that with His
help we can do anything." They also practice guided imagery.

When I was working on the C & H Trucking acquisition, I sat there and imagined the contract and the scratching of the pen on the paper, and I could see the half-chewed cigar in the other man's mouth, the suit he was wearing, the suit I was wearing, and the pressure of his handshake as we agreed on the deal. I imagined that in technicolor and stereophonic sound for about two weeks before the deal.[31]

The work environment is also flexible and somewhat less formally structured than is the case in many business settings. McKinney explains his management style this way:

We really believe in results around here and not in efforts . . . I don't really hold any of my people to a high standard of long hours or worry about how hard they work. There are a lot of people who are so busy preparing to do a tremendous job they never get around to doing it. We operate and compensate on the principle that results count.[32]

The product is a positive work environment supportive of the creative exploration of new ways of doing things—one in which right brain processes like intuition can flourish. As a result, Tyler Corporation is regarded as one of the top five best managed companies in the Southwest. McKinney sums up his philosophy this way, "Just because something has not been done doesn't mean it can't be done. There are no limits."[33]

Government managers have also found that practicing the use of intuition on a regular basis can be helpful in guiding decisions in a whole range of situations—from planning for the future development of a city to putting out the daily fires that come up at city hall. Francis T. Fox, city manager of San Jose, California, relies on intuition as one technique as he tries to guide the development of a grand strategy for the development of the city for the year 2000. Trying to predict the future has become a monumental challenge for city managers. The rate of change has accelerated and there has never been more instability in society. Biophysicist John Platt suggests that there have been more profound changes in the past 40 years than in the previous 600 years combined. In San Jose, the Planning Department, city officials, and a blue ribbon committee of industrial and commercial leaders are trying to meet this challenge through a future planning process called Horizon 2000. Their goal is to avoid the threats of overdevelopment while providing the necessary services to their residents.

City manager Fox describes how he uses intuition integratively with facts to develop the plan for the future.

Good management of human beings involves inspiration and supervision. Under the heading of inspiration comes the intuitive approach to management. It is based upon the major judgment, the past experience, the gut feeling, and more importantly, on the reflective thinking of the manager of a major operation such as the city of San Jose. Albert Einstein acknowledged the importance of this factor in these words, "I believe in intuition and inspiration. Imagination is more important than knowledge, for knowledge is limited whereas imagination embraces the entire world, stimulating progress, giving birth to evaluation. It is strictly speaking a real factor in scientific research."[34]

Randolph J. Forrester, city manager of Wyoming, Ohio, uses a free association technique to tap into his intuitive ability and encourage that of his staff. Essentially, he avoids a logical step-by-step approach to analyzing a given problem. Instead, he approaches any given situation with the attitude that he is willing to try anything and a presumption that there is not a 100% right way to do anything forever. When a creative idea doesn't work, he goes back to the old way or tries another approach. This method, Forrester finds, helps employees feel that they are not stuck with a new idea that doesn't work and yet a positive environment remains in which to keep trying new ideas. Intuitive thinking, he finds, is not only practical in the sense of being a problem-resolution technique, but it is also fun and one of the more psychologically rewarding aspects of management. To see a new approach or idea become a successful, better way to accomplish something is very satisfying.

> This approach has worked for me, and has resulted in a number of unique solutions and approaches. These range from women's intern programs and combined meter reader/animal warden positions to self-insured dental/optical/savings accounts.[35]

William G. McGinnis, city manager of Crescent City, California, believes that the difference between good managers and great managers is their relative ability to make correct decisions in tense or emergency situations. He sees the ability to use intuition to guide decisions under these circumstances as the key factor that separates the good from the best. McGinnis' formula for intuitive decision making is both colorful and suscinct.

> I believe that good intuitive decisions are directly proportional to one's years of challenging experience, plus the number of related and worthwhile years of training and education, all divided by lack of confidence or the fear of being replaced.[36]

In emergency situations, he uses only his intuition. There is not time or information to do otherwise. McGinnis finds in these situations the best decisions are made when he is able to step back from the action for a moment and redirect the adrenaline from his body to his brain. When more time is available and the situation is not so tense, he employs an integrated-intuitive (I-INTU) decision-making style similar to the top managers described in Chapter 2. McGinnis follows ten basic steps.

TABLE 4.5. Steps In An Integrated-Intuitive Management Style

STEP	TECHNIQUE TO USE
1. Make notes outlining the problem, possible solutions, activities to arrive at the solutions, methods to measure the effectiveness of the activities, and projected impacts.	Use combination of right brain and left brain resources. Experience and intuition both helpful.
2. Make preliminary selection of best alternatives.	Integrative-Intuitive with emphasis on the latter.
3. Review Step 1 with key management personnel and, in certain cases, with line personnel.	Use combination of right and left brain skills. Computer analysis, brain-storming, team design based on BMS assessment, meeting room design and color all relevant.
4. Awaken in the middle of the night with alternatives or factors not previously considered.	Meditation can be used. Intuitive predominately. Focus mind on problem before going to sleep, use meditation tape to do so. Jot down solutions when they come to you. Review in morning.
5. Discuss with family, associates, council members, or key persons in the community.	Integrated. Persons selected for input can be based on deductive or inductive decisions. How input is obtained can be by formal or informal means. Techniques in Step 3 could also be used here.
6. Argue both sides of the issue or problem to better understand potential impacts.	Team building based on BMS assessments can make this step most productive, increase chance of missing obvious blind spots. Casual free flowing style helpful here. Structure meeting so input comes from right brain sources first, followed by analysis and critique of left brain sources last, concluding with consensus agreement integrating different perspectives on issues.
7. Refine process in Steps 1 and 2 and possibly redo Steps 3, 5, and 6, before sending up trial balloons.	All of the above.
8. Send up trial balloons by talking to council, newspaper staff, and citizens.	Step 5 methods and techniques repeated. Order may vary.

STEP	TECHNIQUE TO USE
9. Prepare formal proposal for consideration by others (if necessary).	Integrated but probably rely more on left brain analytical steps at this point.
10. Implement decision.	Integrated. How to go about each step will be situational requiring a reliance on both left and right brain techniques as appropriate.

Adapted from William G. McGinnis, "Decision-Making Process," *Public Management* (February, 1983), p. 17. Copyright © 1983 by International City Management Association. Reprinted by permission of *Public Management* and the International City Management Association.

Washoe County, Nevada, has been seeking to develop and use the creative potential in their governmental unit by experimenting with a number of the tools and techniques we have outlined above. Ed Everett, assistant county manager, puts it this way:

> Many of us feel that creativity is something only a few exceptional people like poets, musicians, and scientists have. Hence, we passively accept our noncreative lot in life—our cocoon. Quite the contrary is true however. All of us have the potential to be more creative—we just need practice and training.[37]

The approach they have found to be successful is to start with a small group of ten employees initially composed of department and division heads, a first-line supervisor, an administrative assistant, public health nurse, and the assistant county manager. No agenda was set, and no particular methodology was initially adopted on how to go about improving the creativity of the county government.

At first the group began by focusing on developing their own intuitive skills with the eventual goal of transfering what they learned to the governmental units they worked for. There were some false starts and delays, but in the end after 2 years of work they find they are much more creative than when they started. Through monthly meetings and weekend retreats, the group started working on puzzles found in such materials as Eugene Raudsepp's series of books on creative growth. By working on the puzzles and sharing their solutions, they gained insight into how each group member often blocks creative solutions to problems.

Next, they moved from the puzzles to rigorous brainstorming on hypothetical problems and eventually to actual problems within the county government. They also turned to an outside consultant to assist in this process. Relaxation techniques such as music, art exercises, self-hypnosis, and guided imagery were introduced. They also discussed holistic health and the necessary relationship between mind, body, and spirit. They also examined the science or art of knowledge, acupuncture, reflexology, and iridology. They came to realize that to be truly creative required an integration of both the left and right side of the brain.

The group now believes strongly that creativity is a major skill needed to prevent their county from becoming obsolete. They have learned to look beyond traditionally accepted solutions and not to become trapped in the negative power of group think. Now they also hope to effectively change the total county organization of 1400 employees by forming separate groups of ten, each led initially by members of the original ten.[38]

Certain individuals have also chalked up a success record of using intuition to make decisions—particularly about the future. One example is Alan Vaughan who is considered to be one of the top ten psychics in the country for accuracy as measured by The Central Premonitions Registry in New York City, an organization that keeps a record of predictions about the future. Recently, he competed with four experts in economics to estimate the rate of inflation for the period beginning in 1982. The experts predicted that inflation would be double digit and would accelerate. He predicted correctly that it would subside to 8% by mid-1982. Vaughan said his prediction was based on two steps.

> First, I assumed that the experts might be wrong. Second, I visualized a graph of the coming years' inflation rate and estimated . . . I had no logical data to back up my prediction, but I did experience that gut feeling that told me to pay attention to my mental picture.[39]

Vaughan also believes that intuitive ability can be trained. He recommends a series of exercises to develop your skill—particularly for looking forward and seeing the future. First, select some future development that interests you. Next, relax and let all the logical information drain out of your mind using one or all of the techniques outlined above (for example, meditation). Now, shift your awareness to the future. Set your mind's eye on your target, and estimate how far away in years it might be. Now, ask specific questions that you would like to have answered. Evaluate the answers you receive by giving greater weight to visual cues accompanied by a strong gut feeling in the solar plexus. The same technique can be replicated with a group, such as a group of managers. In this case, group the individual predictions and examine them for any sort of consensus. Then compare the results with the reality outcome as a basis for further skill development, group refinement, and future training exercises. You may even wish to set up two competing groups, one composed of left brain projectors and the other right brain projectors. See for yourself who comes closest to the actual target based on reality testing.

Resources to Help You Develop Your Intuition

There are a number of resources that you will find useful in helping you develop your own intuitive ability as well as that of your organization. We will not try to cite them all here, but give you some guided suggestions to which sources could prove to be most useful—at least initially. (See bibliography for a more complete listing of resources.[40])

First, to develop your cognitive awareness about intuition and your own personal intuitive ability, as well as that of your total organization, we suggest becoming familiar with and take the various test instruments we have outlined earlier (TYMS, Myers-Briggs Type Indicator, Mobius Psi-Q I and II Tests, and Alan Vaughan's Computer Test for Precognitive Ability). We encourage you to study your results, and compare them with your friends' and colleagues'. A similar exercise in your organization would be highly useful at this point. Other indicators of intuitive ability, as well as measure of other brain skills, are also available including handwriting analysis. Examine the work of Charlotte P. Leibel, author of *Change Your Handwriting, Change Your Life,* and *The Journal of Graphoanalysis* published by The International Graphoanalysis Society in Chicago. Having your own handwriting analyzed is strongly recommended.

We also suggest you take other personality and leadership style assessment tests at this point. Perhaps you have previously taken some at work or elsewhere. If so, dig them out and take this opportunity for an overall personal assessment of yourself and your organization's strengths and weaknesses. Remember—this process is like exploring for oil. The more complete the information base about yourself and your organization, the better your chance of striking the paydirt of increased productivity and job satisfaction. Particularly recommended is the "Life Styles Inventory" produced by Human Synergistics in Plymouth, Michigan. This instrument, in graphic form, measures thinking styles of both individuals and organizations, the needs, attitudes, beliefs, and values that cause you to think the way you do. It also reflects the areas in which that thinking affects job performance. Through research Human Synergistics has found that they can accurately predict how a group will score in a problem-solving exercise 80% of the time if they know the results of this test.[41]

Also recommended is Will Schutz's FIRO-B instrument that measures your need structure on three dimensions: inclusion, control, and affection. The test also indicates whether you express these needs actively or passively. The results can be used, along with the findings from other tests above, to properly place you in an organization and position where you are most likely to be productive.[42] For example, previous research has shown that individuals who score high on the intuitive portion of the Myers-Briggs Type Indicator are more likely to do well at creative writing and personal counseling. Similarly, nurses and salespeople score higher on needs for inclusion and affection, while architects score highest in the need for control.[43]

TABLE 4.6. FIRO-B Summary of Personal Need Structure

	INCLUSION	*CONTROL*	*AFFECTION*
Express			
Want			

Adapted and reproduced by special permission of the publisher, Consulting Psychologists Press, Inc., Palo Alto, CA 94306, from *FIRO-B, 1977 Edition* by Will Schutz, copyright © 1967. Further reproduction is prohibited without the Publisher's consent.

You now have a snapshot picture of who you are, how you think, and whether you use your strong suit (whether it be right, left, or integrated brain skills) on the job to make decisions. You should take a look at your tension levels and health statistics at this point. What does it tell you? Are you well aligned personally and on the job? Or, do you have some repair work to do? A complete physical examination using some of the modern health assessment techniques would also be ideal at this stage.

One of the things that constantly amazes me is that individuals and organizations seldom stop to spend this kind of time or effort on self-assessment when it appears to have such a high potential for productivity improvement as well as job satisfaction. Even in those rare cases where some kind of testing or assessment has been completed by an organization, frequently the orientation is really more like a spot oil check than a necessary check for ongoing maintenance and development of our most important resource—human capital.

To help you get an even better handle on who you are, your ability to use intuition to make decisions, and your future potential, it is recommended at this stage that you examine some of the materials available that describe intuitive personalities in greater detail, their different types, characteristics, strengths and weaknesses, and how they can potentially function best in organizational settings. Especially recommended is *People Types and Tiger Stripes: A Practical Guide to Learning Styles*, Gordon Lawrence, *Gifts Differing*, Isabel Briggs Myers and Peter B. Myers, *Please Understand Me: An Essay on Temperament Styles*, David Kinsey and Marilyn Bates, and *Facing Your Type*, George J. Schemel and James A. Borbely.

Next, it would be most helpful to practice some of the synergistic exercises previously outlined. This will help you *internalize*, on an emotional level, how you think and act *in action*. It will give you a better sense of where you go for guidance to make decisions when information is complete and when it is not complete. You will also get a better sense of how well aligned you really are. For example, do you *in fact* rely on your strongest underlying potential skills to make decisions or do you avoid them? Normally, you will also have a little better picture of what your potential is by obtaining the input from your colleagues during the exercises. The synergistic games recommended are Project Planning Situation, Desert Survival Situation, and Par Excellánce. These are all produced by Human Synergistics.

It is now time to examine your immediate career goals and work. Are the goals realistic? Does the job seem to fit you? What kinds of changes (if any) are required, and how might you go about making them? At this point, you might wish to complete the Self Dialogue exercise outlined above. This should help you to get further in touch with *your internal processes* and the role you have played up to now to get you where you are presently—or where you are not *vis-à-vis* your own goals. Now is a good time to pause and reflect again on what you have learned about yourself so far. Relax. Let what you have learned come to your cognitive awareness.

Now go on to the next step in the process of developing your cognitive knowledge about intuition and your ability to use it to make decisions. Review some of the existing literature on intuition, ESP, and psychic phenomena. You will be surprised to learn in the process how many managers use this skill and openly admit doing so. You will also begin to get clues on how other people have learned to work with and develop their intuitive ability further. You may wish to begin with Douglas Dean and John Mihalasky's book called *Executive ESP*. This book outlines how top CEO's of major corporations scored on tests for ESP, and how this skill is linked to a higher profit record. Frances E. Vaughan's book, *Awakening Intuition,* is an excellent and inexpensive paperback book that will give you a firm background on how to develop and use your intuitive ability. You will now probably find it instructive to read Chapter 4, "Zen and the Art of Management" in the bestseller, *The Art of Japanese Management: Applications for American Executives* by Richard Pascale and Anthony Anthos who are faculty members in the business schools of Stanford and Harvard respectively. I also recommend *The Book of Five Rings: The Real Art of Japanese Management* by Miyamoto Musashi.

There are many other books that could be recommended here for a general background and to build your cognitive knowledge. Just a few are *Mind-Reach: Scientists Look at Psychic Ability,* Russel Targ and Harold Puthoff, *Psychic Discoveries Behind the Iron Curtain,* Sheila Ostrander and Lynn Schroeder, *Edgar Cayce on ESP,* Doris Agee, and *Jung, Synchronicity, and Human Destiny,* Ira Progoff. If you wish to get a little more far out exposure to psychic phenomena, look at *Beyond the Body,* Sandra Gibson, *Ahead of Myself: Confessions of a Professional Psychic,* Shawn Robbins, and *Psychics,* which contains in-depth interviews with several well known psychics.

Now you are ready to work on developing your own intuitive skills further. There are mounds of resources to help you in this process. Games and exercises abound in the three book series by Eugene Raudsepp on *Creative Growth.* Jean Houston, the author of *Mind Games,* published a book in 1982 entitled *The Possible Human,* which is, in effect, a course on extending your physical, mental, and creative abilities further. Martin Gardner's book, *Aha!* contains puzzles to exercise and improve your ability to solve problems. The short book by Mark A. Thurston entitled *Understand and Develop Your ESP* focuses on this dimension of your intuitive ability. *Using Your Head* by Stuart B. Litvak explores in some detail how you can develop the brain skills you presently allow to lie dormant. Chapter 11 is devoted exclusively to intuition.

There are a number of other books and resources that outline techniques that you can use to help unlock your intuitive ability. This includes everything from meditation to guided imagery to dream analysis. A best seller by a doctor is Brugh Joy's *Joy's Way.* Another recommended book is *Exploring Inner Space: Awareness Games for All Ages,* Christopher Hills and Deborah Rozman. Meditation exercises for young and old are contained in such books as *Meditation for Children, Joy in the Classroom,* and *Into Meditation Now,* all released by The University of the Trees in Boulder Creek, California. Betty Edward's recent book, *Drawing on the Right Side of the Brain,* outlines techniques for enhancing creative artwork. The techniques she outlines have direct application to style of management as well.

Audio-visual aids also abound, but few are directly linked to applications in management settings. My own materials are an exception in this regard. Four hours of videotape produced for television and workshop use is now available. One program of 2 hours, entitled "Using Intuition to be More Effective at Work and in Your Personal Life," was recently produced by Walt Disney Enterprises in California. Also available is a television interview with Alan Vaughan on "The Use of Intuition in Management," produced in Los Angeles, and a 1-hour workshop for the local chamber of commerce on "Intuitive Management Techniques." Related tapes on how to develop your ESP and psychic skills are also available from such organizations as ARE in Virginia Beach, Virginia, Unity in Unity Village, Missouri, and The University of the Trees in Boulder Creek, California.

If your focus happens to be exclusively on developing your ability to see the future, two sources will be of particular assistance. Alan Vaughan's book, *The Edge of Tomorrow: How to Foresee and Fulfill Your Future,* outlines exercises to practice as does David Loye's *The Knowable Future: A Psychology of Forecasting and Prophecy.* You may also wish to contact such organizations as The Central Premonitions Registry in New York City and The Mobius Group in Los Angeles, California, that are conducting research in this area. You can also take The Mobius Group's Psi-Q II Test which appeared in the October, 1982, issue of *Omni Magazine*. This instrument measures your remote viewing and precognitive ability. Furthermore, you may be interested in examining Alan Vaughan's software computer game called The Psychic Defender. Through practice, you can further increase your precognitive ability.

Finally, you may wish to consider attending a weekend retreat or seminar to work on developing your intuitive ability. Around the country, such programs are regularly offered and recommended selectively as a way to accelerate your own personal development. If you have difficulty locating one satisfactory to you, consult your phone book for a local parapsychological association which should be up to date on current activities. If that is not possible, call the Psychology Department of the nearest university in your area. Usually at least one faculty member is active or aware of such events.

PRACTICING YOUR INTUITION AT WORK

Here are a few hands on games you can try at work as you are developing your intuitive ability further. It might be more fun to try this with some of your coworkers or managers too and keep a record of your successes and failures over time. Meet periodically to discuss how each of you did. Try to identify within yourself those factors that seem to lead to successful predictions and those that do not. Try to strengthen the former and eliminate the latter. One way to help do that is form a team of predictors based on your complementary personality characteristics applying some of the techniques outlined in Chapter 3.

Monthly Forecasts

Whatever your organization, take an activity or performance objective that is considered an important measure of success and that is also reported on a monthly basis. Now, try to predict what that figure will be 1 month out, 2 months out, and so on up to one year. Play this game following these rules:

1. Think of what the figure will be before you go to sleep. Be relaxed about it—just put it in your mind for a moment, toss it around lightly.
2. Play a short meditation tape or engage in some other form of relaxing exercise.
3. If you awaken during the night with a figure, write it down. If not, don't worry about it.
4. When you awaken in the morning, see if you have a figure then. If so, write it down. If not, don't worry about it.

5. Engage in a short meditation exercise before eating breakfast. After doing so, see if you have a figure in your mind. If so, record it. If not, again, don't worry about it.

6. Sometime during the day that is convenient within your work schedule (or just after work), meet with your team partners. Practice a short relaxation exercise and then jot down whatever number "feels" right. Share it with your team. Based on this exchange, either keep that number or change it.

7. Practice these steps every day but don't do it on the weekends unless you really feel comfortable doing so.

8. At the end of the month before the actual monthly figures are released, *rescan* the numbers you have recorded at various times. Again, pick the *one number* from your series of predictions that feels right to you *right then!*

9. Put it in an envelope and seal it.

10. Meet with your team members at the time you normally do each day—or just before lunch. Exchange sealed envelopes. Try now to *predict* the number given to you that is inside the envelope handed to you by a team member. Put it in an envelope and seal it. Now go to lunch, and open the envelopes. Whoever is closest to the *actual monthly forecast* and who is most accurate in predicting a team member's own prediction gets the free lunch or some other prize.

11. Keep a record of successes and failures for six months or so. Now, sit down seriously one day at work and exchange all the available information each of you has such as MBTI test data, techniques used to predict, personal exercises followed, things each of you has learned about your own feelings. This process should give you concrete clues as to why some members in the group are *consistently* more accurate in their predictions than other members. This will help you and your organization in several practical ways: to identify those managers who should be assigned to problem-solving matters where intuitive skills would be particularly valued; to identify specific work-related exercises that can be used to help you and other managers develop your right brain skills more effectively; and to assist everyone in learning how to build team skills more effectively which, together, are most likely to lead to greater productivity overall.

Supervisor–Subordinate

Take people who are presently working in some form of regular day-to-day supervisor-and-subordinate relationship (examples are doctor–nurse, boss–secretary, president–district manager, foreman–assembly line worker). Follow these steps identified as an "experimental exercise" within your organization, but administered by a person inside or outside the formal setting competent to act as a facilitator.

1. Start with 30-minute exchanges made up of 15 minutes each.

2. Ask each of the two participants to sit facing each other. Tell them to hold hands and close their eyes. Now ask them to think of words like *cooperation, support, help,* and *assistance.*

3. Start with the supervisor asking the subordinate the simple question, "How do you feel I can do my job more effectively?" You record the answers while the supervisor listens.

4. Now reverse the process with the subordinate asking the same question. Again, record in the same manner.

5. When this process has been completed, ask each person to thank the other person for his suggestions. Ask each of them to acknowledge that he will reflect on what was said and report back next time.

6. Use the next session for an exchange where each person can freely outline what he has accepted or rejected and why. Again, at the end of the session, ask each person to thank the other for his input.

7. After this process has been completed at least twice, spend one session where you ask each person separately and then jointly what he has learned *about himself first,* and *then about* the other person.

8. Clear, precise, and measurable indicators should be now available showing that the process is not only productive, but should be implemented throughout your organization. If you think it would be helpful, you might also wish to consider awarding some kind of prize or giving some form of personal recognition for the suggestions which had the greatest impact on organizational and/or personal productivity.

Create Your Own Game

One of the best exercises you can use to practice developing your intuition for use at work is to create your own game related to management problem solving.

Think about the organizational and personal goals that you have at work. Think about the work environment you would like to experience in reality that would be conducive to achieving them. Ask a coworker or management team to do the same. Then share your respective lists. Next, create your own playfair games for yourself and your colleagues to help bring you to the *actual place* you *want to be together.*

Now let us turn to the last chapter of this book. Here we will examine some of the most innovative work presently being conducted to apply right brain techniques, such as intuition, to make actual management decisions in modern day organizations. We will also explore how these applications are likely to increase in the future, and how this process is likely to hold the key to increasing America's productivity for the balance of the century and beyond.

5

The Most Innovative
Use of Intuition
in Modern Organizations

Until recently, the world was divided into two totally different cultural perspectives which conditioned how organizations functioned. In the Western World, the orientation has essentially been predominantly left brain. It has been the dominant belief that men and women, through the objective application of skills and techniques of their own creation, could dominate the forces of nature and channel them for their own purposes. The tools used have been quantitative and impersonal and directed to the achievement of so-called rational decisions. The computer, which has grown in power and capability, has been enlisted to serve in the cause. Now we are all familiar with the language that has sprung from this approach to life: PPBS, ZBB, MBO, PERT, cost-benefit analysis, and projections are just a few familiar terms we hear every day. Competition as opposed to cooperation has also been stressed as the predominant management style. The way to the top, then, is to be impersonal, rational, and competitive.

Management education and training programs across the country have naturally emphasized this approach to life. Recently, Ralph Z. Sorenson, now president and CEO of Barry Wright Corporation, a manufacturer of computer related accessories and other diversified industrial products, put it this way:

> Years ago when I was a young assistant professor at the Harvard Business School, I thought that the key to developing managerial leadership lay in raw brain power. I thought the role of business schools was to develop future managers who knew all about the various functions of business: to teach them how to define problems succinctly, analyze these problems and

89

identify alternatives in a clear, logical fashion, and finally, to teach them to make an intelligent decision.[1]

But, he has gradually tempered his thinking by living and working outside the United States, by serving as a college president, and now also as a company president. What he now believes is essential is not only an executive with all of the left brain skills that management programs like Harvard and Stanford produce, but also leadership skills which he defines as a capacity to "understand and be sensitive to people and be able to inspire them toward the achievement of a common goal." He also believes that effective managers must be broad human beings with a sense of courage and integrity who have the ability to make positive things happen.

> An effective manager not only understands the world of business but also has a sense of the cultural, social, political, historical, and international aspects of life and society. This suggests that exposure to the liberal arts and humanities should be part of every manager's education.[2]

This brings us to the second cultural orientation in the world—the Eastern. In countries like Japan, China, and India the belief is that humanity should learn to work in harmony with nature and with each other. The focus is inductive, and right brain skills of management such as intuition are emphasized. The focus is more on achieving methods of cooperation (integrative brain skill applications) than competition. The way to get to the top is to be personal, inductive, and cooperative.

We are familiar with the language of this orientation popularized by the 1983 hit movie *Gandhi* (consciousness). We are also familiar with the management success stories that have been popularized in such books as *The Japanese Art of Management,* and the successful transference of some of these techniques to the United States. The Sharp Manufacturing Company of America story in Memphis, Tennessee, is just one example where product quality and overall plant productivity have been improved dramatically under recent Japanese management.[3]

Now to be sure, each cultural and management orientation derived thereby has its strengths and limitations. But *integrated* together, we have the management potential that Ralph Sorenson longs for above, the productivity we are capable of, and the satisfaction in life that we all desire. We have the I-INTU manager—receptive to input of both facts and feelings, sensitive to the needs of others, and with a capacity through intuition of integrating input received into a highly productive organization that is satisfying to its members. We have an organization where cooperation is both possible and practically productive, and where competition is channeled in a manner that is not destructive. Shigem Okada, head of Mitsukoshi, Japan's largest department store, put it this way:

> Our company's success is due to our adoption of the West's pragmatic management combined with the spiritual intuitive aspects of the East.[4]

What we are talking about here is a *change in the consciousness* of all world cultures and organizations therein—including our own. What we are arguing for is an awareness of how we each have personal and cultural traits and perspectives which *integrated together* have the potential for high productivity and a more satisfying life for us all. We are arguing for a restructuring of our current management education and training programs across the country (and around the world) so that right brain as well as left brain skills are taught with *equal emphasis* and *integrated* into an overall management curriculum appropriate for the organizations and world society of the future. We have tried to show step-by-step in this book how this can be achieved in a practical way.

We are not alone in making this call for change. Recently for example, Derek C. Bok, president of Harvard University, urged a reform of the law school curriculum across the country. Noting that the left brain training characteristics of law schools have produced many triumphs (by learning to think deductively "like a lawyer"), Bok argues that it has also helped to produce a legal system that is among the most expensive and least efficient in the world. In part, this is due to the fact that the present educational training lawyers receive emphasizes legal combat rather than the gentler arts of reconciliation and accommodation where right brain and integrative applications would be most appropriate. Bok continues:

> Over the next generation, I predict, society's greatest opportunities will lie in tapping human inclinations toward collaboration and compromise rather than stirring our proclivities for competition and rivalry.[5]

Frank Rose makes a similar argument in his 1983 article in *Esquire Magazine* concerning the education and training of engineers in America. He states:

> . . . a postindustrial society requires more than just a lot of engineers. It requires engineers with the vision and the foresight to see where they are going and the verbal capacity to tell us about it. . . . Our institutions . . . are not developing the integrative functions required for the thoughtful application of complex systems.[6]

The 1983 report of the Committee on the Future of California State University states that one way our future management leaders (in whatever field) can be more effectively trained is to recognize and integrate both left and right brain learning styles in our education programs. Noting that learning styles by individual vary, and that new teaching methods appropriate for each style need to be developed, the Report concludes, ". . . Intuition and perhaps extrasensory perception may have been validated as a means of reaching and training both the conscious and unconscious mind."[7]

Evidence abounds everywhere that managers in both the private and public sectors are becoming increasingly aware that *there is a better way* of orienting themselves and their organization that pays off in terms of practical results and that also *feels* good. Many of these managers are proceeding to take matters into their own hands, and simply implement a better way. Take Morris J. Siegel, cofounder of Celestial Seasonings and a self-made millionaire. Recently, he was faced with the decision of launching an advertisement campaign that directly attacked Lipton—a competitive product. After a long bike ride listening to consciousness tapes, he decided to scrap the entire campaign. He explained, "Basically, I was saying that if it doesn't follow the golden rule, I don't want to participate in it. We've never made any money bad-mouthing anyone else."[8] Siegel's approach is simple. It is possible to move sales from $28.5 million in 1983 to $100 million by 1990 without giving up his principles. He emphasizes hard work and incentive rewards for each employee, as well as heavy spending on employee and management training (for example, listening to employees). Siegel explains his philosophy, "You want your people to grow, and this is a positive reinforcement of your people as human beings . . . It's also cheaper to train people and build them, rather than getting rid of them while you're constantly looking for the ideal person." He describes himself as "very Christian" though not a churchgoer. "We're not interested in making our fortunes by cursing the darkness, but by making excellent products."[9]

At Control Data, vice president Bill Hultgren has made a pact with employees guaranteeing that the company will follow through on all reasonable suggestions to enhance the organizational culture.

> We needed sustained improvement in productivity, but we knew that the old ways of making changes don't stick to the ribs. We knew we needed to change the whole company climate.[10]

Hultgren and his department looked at the known attributes of high-performance companies: few levels of management, performance based rewards, job security, environment of personal growth, and clear communications. Then they established a policy committee to answer the question, "What should it be like around here?" The suggested changes in policy and structure that came out of this process have been so useful and specific that 2000 employees in engineering services are now refining their own organizations. Hultgren notes, "They are creating a climate of self-reliance, therefore changing the destiny of the organization."[11] The women that are rising rapidly in their professions across America today also exude this new consciousness. Take, for example, Lea Haller. At 29 she is the leader of a budding multicontinental cosmetics empire. Lea Haller Cosmetics. Asked to explain her formula for success, she speaks of "the laws of the universe." What does she mean? Samples she gives are:

> Your thinking, your attitude, is *everything* . . . Decide what you want, create it in your mind, then go out and make it happen. It will. The first step is to be in tune with yourself and the universe . . . My company is successful because it allows each individual to do what he or she really enjoys doing, something that's fun for them . . . But, first you must know inside yourself what that something is. Once you do, the only thing left is to go for it.[12]

Part of this transformation in management consciousness includes the highly innovative introduction, use, and training of such right brain skills as intuition into organizational decision making. So far, the results clearly suggest that the use of intuition in management is one key for increasing American productivity in the decades ahead. We have previously discussed several examples of where managers are regularly using intuition as part of their effort to increase productivity (both personally and in their organizations as a whole). Here, we will focus on describing more fully, selected examples of some of the *most innovative* applications used or being experimented with at the present time.

Innovative Use of Intuition in Organizations

On a national level, one of the most innovative organizations is The Mobius Society based in Los Angeles, California. Headed by Stephan A. Schwartz, the organization specializes in the use of right brain skills to solve a variety of organizational problems and also conducts very significant research projects in the field of parapsychology. Supported by corporate clients, individual contributions, service fees, and publication royalties, The Mobius Society is currently engaged in a series of projects that have received national attention.

One project involves using a team of recognized psychics to implement a modified Delphi technique for guiding archeological dig expeditions as well as performing other client assignments. A book, entitled *The Alexandria Project,* was just released exploring their technique in detail.[13] Another of their major projects has been a national survey published through *Omni Magazine* in which they have tested over 18,000 respondents concerning their psychic ability (Psi). Two test instruments have been developed. The first originally published in *Omni Magazine* in October, 1981, tested for individual brain styles (left, right, and integrative) as well as the psychic ability to see the future by requiring the respondent to pick a target not yet generated randomly by a computer. They also asked a series of other questions covering personal characteristics of the respondents in order to determine if there is any significant correlation between the traits and psychic ability.[14]

Their conclusions were published in the November, 1982, issue of *Omni*. They found that some magazine readers who took the test were able to score better than chance on guessing numbers *precognitively* that were later generated randomly. They were also able to locate super psychics, those who had very high scores on the precognitive portion of the test. This could be a significant find all by itself in view of recent Russian research that indicates that only one out of every 200,000 people have this ability. One of the future agenda projects of The Mobius Society is to enlist the services of such gifted psychics to help work on solving major problems facing our nation.[15]

Although they did not find any discernible difference by sex as we did in our national testing, many of their other findings are consistent with ours. They did find, for example, that brain styles appear to vary by occupational specialty. The highest number of right brain people were found to be working in the category called "artistic" which includes journalists, musicians, and graphic designers. Similarly, the highest number of left brain problem solvers work in the category classified as "investigating physical, biological, and cultural phenomena" which includes computer operators, engineers, and physicians.[16]

In October, 1982, The Mobius Society published their second test that measures your ability to remote view (the ability to see distant locations or events with the aid of psychic power alone). Again they also asked a series of personality profile questions.[17] This test is one indicator of your ability to see the future. Remote viewing can also be used to increase your capacity to see the future. The "Feedback Report" that respondents get suggests some of the potential application this skill can have in daily organizational settings.

> Before going into a meeting, or visiting a place you have never been before, stop and take a few minutes to remote view it. Make note of your major impressions, including both physical descriptions and the personalities of unknown people involved. After the meeting or visit, compare your perceptions with what actually took place. Note the points where you were accurate and get a sense of how you experienced, or felt, correct perceptions. Gradually you will find your accuracy rate going up.[18]

At this point, it is interesting to note the contrasting evaluation by the United States and Russia on the predicted value of research of this type. Leonid L. Vasiliev, winner of the Lenin Peace Prize, states, "The discovery of the energy underlying extrasensory perception will be the equivalent of the discovery of atomic energy."[19] At home, on the other hand, government expenditures for research in this area are very small, and industry's contributions are virtually nonexistent.

David Loye, cofounder of the Institute for Future's Forecasting, sees the value of using intuitive input from the right side of the brain to project future events that are likely to affect organizational survival. Noting that many of the traditional left brain techniques alone have not demonstrated a very successful track record for projecting the future of the economy, for example, he has been conducting a major national research project which involves using intuitive input as well.[20] Loye has developed a "1983 Knowable Future Study" that asks respondents to predict a series of future events by September 1, 1983, concerning presidential elections, the economy, and world issues, both of a short-term and long-term nature. The test also contains a brain/mind profile that will be used, as in The Mobius Society studies, to correlate personality characteristics with ability to intuitively predict the future accurately.[21]

Group intuition or "The Delphi Technique" as it is more commonly known uses right brain as well as left brain input to reach predictions about the future. The Rand Corporation in California and the military have practically applied this approach for years. However, Alan Vaughan has suggested that this process could be refined and made *even more accurate* by loading expert groups to include those who score very high on intuitive tests or other similarly psychic measures.[22] Loye's own research has suggested that people who seem to have the greatest ability to predict the future are "balanced brained" or integrated, which is consistent with our own national testing of top managers. That is, managers who tend to draw on both halves of the brain equally turn out to be better predictors than those who are more exclusively right or left brain dominant.[23] In a 1979 study, Loye also found that executives were using different kinds of forecasting models depending on their brain style in the early stages of deciding which film in the movie industry would be successful. These findings are similar to my observations and testing at Walt Disney Enterprises where left brain financeers and right brain imagineers often went by each other when it came to organizational communication. Loye again found in this study that integrated managers had a better track record of predicting industry success. He notes the practical implications of these findings for organizations, "Not only can big think-tanks which routinely grapple with problems of national and global scope, sharpen their predictions, but we can make more accurate predictions about events in our own lives as well."[24]

Robert Eggert also uses a group intuition technique to better predict the economy. Relying on 46 economists around the country, he calls them every month for each of their individual predictions. Then he averages the various projections along with his own to make a blue chip consensus forecast for his clients. So far during his 6 years of activity, this method has proven to be more likely to be on target than individual forecasts.[25] In fact, a recent study of 79 forecasters by the National Bureau of Economic Research in Cambridge, Massachusetts, concludes that over the recent 11-year period, group averages "have tracked actual changes better" than typical individual forecasters.[26] Each month Eggert also asks his expert source group to predict several special questions such as what the Federal Reserve Board's performance might be.

As noted earlier, Alan Vaughan has outlined a series of steps for developing your skill for predicting the future intuitively in order to help guide management decisions. Training your intuition can also be fun. Vaughan's microcomputer game, The Psychic Defender is now readily available for use on Apple models. The game is designed to increase a player's awareness of internal signals that have been shown to accompany accurate prediction of the future. Practice with the game will increase your accuracy rate of prediction. The player uses a radarlike beam to sense which of six target areas will be chosen by the Apple computer at random. After the player presses a fire button, the computer generates the actual vs. predicted target. The game automatically records the top ten game scores. Only the player's intuitive mind power limits how high he or she can score.[27]

Inferential Focus (IF), a firm located in New York City, specializes in using intuitive techniques to scan current periodicals for blue chip clients and predict the trend of future events on the basis of this analysis. Often referred to as the CEO's CIA, the one commonality among their clients is a mind-set that values the intuitive thought processes for reaching major decisions. IF analyzes 175 periodicals on a regular basis to intuitively identify unexpected events. As Bennett W. Goodspeed, the late senior partner of IF points out, their process of broadly scanning what appears to be a group of unrelated periodicals and events is critical because "early indicators of change often first show up outside the area that will be most severely impacted."[28] When IF has reached a conclusion, they transmit it to their clients via monthly phone conversations as well as quarterly meetings. This approach is used because it provides not only an opportunity to immediately transmit early signs of change, but also, over time, creates a consciousness with their clients that greatly improves their individual skills of observation and interconnective creativity.

One example of IF's ability to spot an early development and interpret it properly using intuition was Saudi Arabia's sudden change in requirements concerning all incoming computerized freight. Containers, which in the past had measured 40 feet and contained two doors, were now required to be scaled back to just 20 feet and have four doors. Not only that, the Saudis went from 20% inspection of all containers to 100%. IF's inference was that the Saudis were worried about illegal arms shipments and the security of the country. IF also concluded that the Saudis, because of these concerns, would switch some of their wealth into gold, which would, in turn, have a positive effect on the gold price.[29] As the futurist Sam Wilson stated, this demonstrates the following:

> Environmental sensitivity will be a key to strategic success. In such an uncertain and uncharted environment, sensitive and continuous monitoring of external change becomes the corporation's vital sensing mechanism, its essential early-warning system. Like radar, this monitoring system must scan the whole horizon and operate continuously, tracking the blips on the screen, sorting out real from ghost images, checking out forecasts on an incremental basis.[30]

The innovative use of intuition to guide decision making is increasingly prevalent at all levels of the public sector as well. We have already given a number of case examples in previous chapters. In addition, it is worth noting here that such organizations as the International City Management Association have recently featured a whole issue of their journal, *Public Management,* to creativity with the lead article my own work on "The Use of Intuition in Public Management.[31] This is not a short-term interest on their part. For example, their 1982 national conference speaker was Marilyn Grey, who spoke on creative thinking including the use of intuition. In 1981 at the same conference, Roger Von Oech was featured concerning the subject of the mind as a management tool.[32] In fact, it is revealing to review Willis W. Harman's 1980 address to the same group where he noted:

> George Washington gave instructions to his orderly not to be disturbed during the darkest period of the revolutionary war. Washington wanted to turn his deep problems over to his creative, intuitive part of his mind. . . . By his own testimony, George Washington used that kind of insight to guide his decisions throughout his presidency. So did Abraham Lincoln, among others. The founding fathers thought this was so important that they tried to remind us of it on the back of the dollar bill. There you will find an unfinished pyramid with an eye over the top of it. The meaning of this symbol is thousands of years old. The structure is not complete, whether it is the individual's life or the nation, until the all seeing eye is in the capstone position, until this creative, intuitive part of our mind is playing a major role in guiding our decisions.[33]

Selected organizations are now emerging with the awareness of the power of intuitive skills for guiding decisions. One example is Psychic Enterprises, Inc., located in Los Angeles, California. Their services include "advising clients on financing, associates' honesty, banking, management, and complex business situations up to and including acquisitions and mergers." They indicate "the psychic ability of our associates is the basis of our service. By choosing and combining the talents of many psychics working as a team, we produce startlingly accurate reports for our clients.[34]

Innovative Research and Teaching

It is increasingly clear that the growing use of intuition in organizational decision making is reaching the attention of major publishing houses and the public in turn. One example is J. P. Tarcher Inc., of Los Angeles. Always at the forefront of publishing books in fields related to brain research, consciousness, and psychic phenomena, they released a new book in late 1983 by Philip Goldberg entitled *The Intuitive Edge*.[35] This book attempts to explain intuition, to suggest a model of how the intuitive mind works, and it offers a variety of ways to improve one's intuition in decision-making and problem-solving situations. Of course, my own book is another example. One of the major differences between this book and Goldberg's is that mine is based on actual field testing of managers nationally. It is also a much more detailed description of how to use intuition in specific management situations.

Signs are also now appearing that even "the establishment" management education programs across the country such as Harvard and Stanford University are awakening to the importance of intuition as a practical tool for decision making. Perhaps the most innovative course developed so far is offered at Stanford. Developed by Michael Ray and Rochelle Myers, the course is called "Creativity in Business."[36] Included is a heavy treatment of the use of intuition in decision making, including guest speakers from business who proudly admit that they use it on a regular basis to reach *their major decisions!* One student wrote in an analysis of the course:

> You emphasized a new and powerful way of experiencing the self and essence. I'm pleased that I learned how to manage a whole new side of me. The management of the intuitive side along with the analytical side should be an optimum combination.[37]

Leading Edge Bulletin, which regularly monitors innovative approaches to organizational management, has also identified the training work conducted by Innovation Associates of Framingham, Massachusetts. Peter Senge, a MIT assistant professor, is training managers on the use of intuition in management. His research indicates that effective leaders share certain abilities that transcend individual personality and style. They envision a desired state of affairs much like Morris J. Siegel of Celestial Seasonings does. They communicate this vision so that others align with it. Then they design organizational structures that focus efforts toward realizing the vision. They also consciously maintain the direction when obstacles arise—or change direction when necessary. Finally, they master a sense of the overall dynamics of the system. The leader's vision, Senge says, is the vehicle for transmitting company purpose. Whatever the vision, it must "capture people's hearts." Senge notes that this vision is not solely of the intellect:

> The vision that a true leader articulates essentially derives from a different source. It is based on a sensitive attunement to the forces in a system—a real sense of where things are going, of what sort of futures are possible. This sense is not merely based on past behavior but on a deep *intuitive* understanding of a system.[38]

To create change from within the system, intuitive leaders find leverage points. These are small, nonobvious interventions that alter fundamental patterns. Their importance, Senge notes, stems from the insight that systems are not linear. Problems having the most obvious symptoms in marketing and sales, for example, may have causes in shipping or production. In this case, pressure on marketing personnel could make matters worse in the long run. Senge believes that "those who carry the vision of their organization and are sensitive to intuitive insight will be the leaders of the future."[39] Seeking to have an impact on the emerging leadership of tomorrow, Senge and his associates train managers in such organizations as the American Leadership Forum, founded in 1981 to encourage and develop more responsible and effective public leadership in the country.[40]

Finally, I would be remiss not to mention my own research and workshop training on the use of intuition in management. This book has summarized much of my key research so far and also outlined some of my suggestions on how intuition can be used in management settings to guide decisions. I have also outlined how you (and your organization) can go about identifying this skill and develop it for further daily use at work and in your personal life. In the workshops and organizational consulting I do throughout the country, I go through these suggested steps and have participants work on real problems that they are faced with *at that very moment.* But, I go further. I try to demonstrate *on the spot* through my own readings that psychic ability can be developed and eventually used to make management decisions more productive. After all, if I, who started this journey trained primarily on the left have learned to tap into and develop my right side of the brain also, then I ought to be able to demonstrate that fact. That is what I call "reality testing." The whole message of this book is that *you can do it too!*[41]

Postscript

You have traveled with me through this book from my left brain origins over to the development of my right brain skills, and back again as I have sought to integrate the two. I have tried to share with you what I perceive to be the practical implications in management of developing your own capabilities in a similar manner. That is, if you are presently highly skilled on the left, work to expand your skills on the right as well and try to *integrate* the two sides of your capabilities. If you are presently highly skilled on the right, work in the opposite direction.

I have also tried to suggest the changes I feel we need to make in the training of our future management leadership in whatever field. Namely, it seems to me that formal academic and in-house training programs in organizations of all types would be far more productive than they presently are if they would do one thing—move quickly now to place as much emphasis on developing right brain management skills as they presently are on left brain skills. Furthermore, a move needs to be made now to *integrate* both left and right brain skill development into an overall management curriculum appropriate for the organizations and world society of the future.

In leaving you now, I would like to share with you a transcript of a tape made by Alan Vaughan for me on May 7, 1982—*long before* Prentice-Hall had indicated any interest in publishing my book. Vaughan, you will recall, is the gifted psychic from California whose work I have frequently cited throughout this book. I am sharing this tape with you because I think it suggests better than anything I have said so far what power there is on the right side of our capabilities—if we will only work to get in touch with it, and *integrate* what we learn into our day-to-day life.

101

TAPE MADE WITH ALAN VAUGHAN
ON MAY 5, 1982*

After taking in his hands the ring I wear on my left hand, he began.

Vaughan: Why don't I start with some things I already know about you and get them out of the way? I think I know that you worked as a management consultant. If you haven't you will. Now I'm seeing you shifting your position at California State Long Beach. In the fall, this will be. The emphasis of your work will be shifting from there. Occasionally you may teach something there, but your home base is moving I believe. And it will be . . . to a small institute. Oh—I think you will do three papers. And my feeling is that—you may not want to hear this—that your plans for the book will be extended somewhat.

Agor: Delayed you mean?

Vaughan: Yes, I think you will be doing a first draft of maybe a few chapters, but I think you are going to want to include more information based on some interviews and new studies that are being done. So, it's going to take a bit longer than you think right now.

Agor: Do you still see it coming out though?

Vaughan: Yes—I certainly do! And it looks like it's a hard cover . . . at least initially.

Agor: Do you see Tarcher publishing it?

Vaughan: Tarcher?

Agor: Yes, because I've almost had a feeling that I'm being guided to them.

Vaughan: Well, I'm not sure about that.

Agor: Okay.

Vaughan: I wonder if it might be something more like Prentice-Hall—a company that deals more with a list of technical titles. Tarcher is all pop. And I think you will be doing a lot of traveling in the fall to Washington. Certainly, to consult about a training program for an agency there.

Agor: What kind of reception do you see for the book?

Vaughan: Boy, it seems to me being used something like a textbook for several small groups, and then it's going into paper edition. I guess a quality paperback, having a pretty good success. Boy—this sounds far too optimistic to trust, but the figure I just got was 165,000 copies. It seems excessive but. . . .

Agor: I don't know, boy, when you get in that textbook market.

Vaughan: Well—it's not like an undergraduate textbook. That's where the money is. Your book is more like a graduate school book. I think training programs which are not particularly affiliated with universities . . . companies' organizational development. I think you will be working with a large company. I'm thinking of something on the

*Quote from verbatim transcript of precognitive tape predicting publication of book by Prentice-Hall, Inc. prepared by Alan Vaughan for author on May 5, 1982, permission granted by Alan Vaughan, President, Enterprising Ideas, Glendale, California and author of *The Edge of Tomorrow*.

order of IBM—maybe not for the whole Company, but one division of it developing a training program for their employees. It's like a two or three week program they will be going through. But I see the location in Southern California or the Southwest.

Agor: This institute that you see me going to in the fall—is it in Southern California?

Vaughan: I believe so. I think it's in southern California, but I'm not sure where it is. I'm not sure that the institute even exists yet. But, it might well be something, or a new program being created from an established organization—creating a new separate program or institute.

Agor: Could it be something I set up myself?

Vaughan: Oh yes—it could very well be.

Agor: Because I have been thinking about it.

Vaughan: Although I think there are some other people involved in it . . . two or three people. I see you going through a study program of your own, fairly intensive—a situation in which you are trying various kinds of things—kind of impossible things, and having quite good success with this. And being quite amazed at the kinds of things you are able to do. I may be projecting here, but I wonder if I might be connected with that somehow.

Agor: Could be.

Vaughan: Like November or so. I think you will be very good at doing impossible things. [Lots of laugher on both parts!]

Agor: There are lots of things that are potentially out there that could make that come to pass—like the September change and so on. It's quite feasible. I've been giving some thought to it because as I've been going on this project, I have a sense myself that something is coming. I don't have any vision exactly of what, but I have a feeling of "don't worry about it." I keep getting that message. It's kind of like it will all unfold in time.

Vaughan: I think you are right. I think September, the economy is going to start improving quite a bit. . . .

As you will note, I felt J. P. Tarcher would publish this book. Vaughan specifically named Prentice-Hall. Five weeks *after* he made this tape, Saul Cohen, Senior Editor at Prentice-Hall, contacted me. He wrote:

You'll be happy to hear that all your various letters and submissions have finally come to rest in a single place—this office. I have gone through all the material, including all the letters you wrote trying to track this thing down, and now a single mind has a pretty good idea of what you are about.

I like your idea for a book. . . . But where is the book? I need a complete outline—a chapter outline and a sample chapter or two to make a presentation to the editorial board in the Trade Division. . . . Can you work something up along these lines that I may take under consideration? . . .

In the nonce, I will retain the numerous letters you wrote while acting as your own detective and ask that you return your c.v., endorsements, and article, together with the chapter outline and sample chapters when you have something to show.

Nearly 1 year later, I sent him the complete book manuscript. (You will recall Vaughan suggested there would be some delay including a job relocation that came to pass.) On June 25, 1983, I received a book contract offer in the mail, and publication is scheduled in the spring of 1984 in both hardcover and paperback—just as Vaughan predicted. An amazing number of other predictions Vaughan made in the tape have come to pass—or are still unfolding. I am sure there are those on the left who will find fault with various aspects of this experiment. But, I say to you, call it what you will . . . it worked didn't it? Believe me, it's been a fun trip too. Try it—you might like it!

Remember what the famous psychologist, Carl G. Jung, told his profession in 1919 at a London meeting, "I shall not commit the fashionable stupidity of regarding everything I cannot explain as a fraud!"

Glossary

Clairvoyance. Extrasensory perception of objects or objective events.

Extrasensory Perception (ESP). Experience of, or response to, a target object, state, event, or influence without sensory contact.

Intuition. A way of knowing, recognizing the possibilities in any situation. Extrasensory perception, clairvoyance, and telepathy are part of the intuitive function.

Parapsychical, Parapsychological (PSI). Extrasensorimotor exchange with the environment. Psi includes ESP, PK, and intuition.

Parapsychology. The branch of science that deals with Psi communication.

Precognition. Prediction of future events (random events), the occurrence of which cannot be inferred from present knowledge.

Psi Phenomena. Occurrences that result from the operation of Psi.

Psychokinesis (PK). The extramotor aspect of Psi. A direct (mental) influence exerted by the subject on an external physical object, process, or condition.

Significance. A numerical result is significant when it equals or surpasses a criteria or degree of chance probability: normally either odds of at least 5 in 100 or 1 in 100.

Synchronicity. When two or more events take place at a given moment of time without either one having caused the other but with a distinctly meaningful relationship existing between them beyond the possibilities of coincidence.

Telepathy. ESP of the mental state or activity of another person.

Notes

PREFACE

[1]Douglas Dean, J. Mihalasky, S. Ostrander, and L. Schroeder, *Executive ESP* (Englewood Cliffs, NJ: Prentice-Hall, Inc., 1974).

[2]The appendix and bibliography contain some of the major instruments, tools, and general sources that I found useful for developing your intuition. Chapters 3 and 4 of this book describe how some of these resources can be used practically to guide management decisions on a daily basis.

CHAPTER 1

[1]See William Taggart and Daniel Robey, "Minds and Managers: On the Dual Nature of Human Information Processing and Management," *Academy of Management Review* (vol. 6, no. 2, 1981), pp. 187–195.

[2]For a recent treatment of both left and right brain approaches in management, see Thomas Vocino and Jack Rabin, *Contemporary Public Administration* (New York: Harcourt Brace Jovanovich, Inc., 1981), pp. 380–390.

[3]Henry Mintzberg, "Planning on the Left Side and Managing on the Right," *Harvard Business Review* (July/August, 1976), pp. 49–58.

[4]Thomas Peters and Robert Waterman, *In Search of Excellence* (New York: Harper & Row, 1983).

[5]See for example Robert B. Denhardt, "Managerial Intuition," *MBA* (February/March, 1979), pp. 13–19; and Camile Cates, "Beyond Muddling: Creativity," *Public Administration Review* (vol. 39, no. 6, November/December, 1979), pp. 527–531.

[6]Mortimer R. Feinberg and Aaron Levenstein, "How Do You Know When to Listen to Your Intuition?", *The Wall Street Journal* (June 21, 1982), p. 16. Reprinted by permission of Dow Jones and Company, Inc.

[7]Bennett W. Goodspeed, "Different Styles of Analysis Imperative to Business: More Often Than Not, Intuition, Not Numbers, Tells the Real Story," *American Banker* (November 9, 1981), and Michael P. Sullivan, "The Intuitive Manager Makes A Quiet Comeback," *American Banker* (March 16, 1983), p. 4.

[8]See for example The Editors, *Harvard Business Review: On Human Relations* (New York: Harper & Row, 1979); Eugene Raudsepp, "Trust That Hunch," *Success* (August, 1982); "How Intuitive Are You?",

New Woman Magazine (May, 1982); Stuart B. Litvak, "Like Sagging Muscles, Intuition Can Be Developed" and Shawn Robbins as told to Milton Pierce, "Those Subtle Little Voices Within," *New Woman Magazine* (October, 1982), pp. 64–68.

[9]Eric N. Berg, "Zen and the Stanford Business Student," *The New York Times* (January 30, 1983), p. 9.

[10]Douglas Dean et. al., *Executive ESP* (Englewood Cliffs, N.J.: Prentice-Hall, Inc. 1974).

[11]Jerry Carroll, "Over-Achievers Swarm to this Exotic Class," *San Francisco Chronicle* (February 17, 1983), p. 46. © *1983 San Francisco Chronicle*. Used by permission.

[12]Cited by Bennett W. Goodspeed, *op. cit.* © 1981, reprinted by permission of *American Banker.*

[13]Ibid. © 1981, reprinted by permission of *American Banker.*

[14]Interview with J. W. Marriott, Jr., as reported by Patrice Steadman, "Hotel Chief Tells How to Survive," *El Paso Times* (November, 1982). Reprinted by permission of The El Paso Times, Inc.

[15]Bryce Nelson, "Management Revolution Urged for Auto Industry," *Los Angeles Times* (July 27, 1982), pp. 1 and 15.

[16]See for example John Naisbitt, "The New Economic and Political Order of the 1980s," *Opinions and Trends* (Yankelovich, Skelly, and White, 1981); and the articles of Alvin Toffler and Willis W. Harman in the special issue of *Public Management* (January-February, 1980), pp. 2–7. Copyright © 1980 by International City Management Association. Reprinted with permission of *Public Management* and The International City Management Association.

[17]Robert Zager and Michael P. Rosow, eds., *The Innovative Organization: Productivity Programs in Action* (Elmsford, N.Y.: Pergamon Press, Inc., 1982).

[18]Laurie McGinley, "Forecasters Overhaul Models of Economy in Wake of 1982 Errors," *The Wall Street Journal* (February, 1983), pp. 1 and 20.

[19]Frances E. Vaughan, *Awakening Intuition* (Garden City, N.Y.: Anchor Books, 1979). Excerpt from *Awakening Intuition* by Frances Vaughan, copyright © 1979 by Frances Vaughan, reprinted by permission of Doubleday & Co., Inc.

[20]*Webster's New World Dictionary* (Cleveland, Ohio: William Collins Publishers, Inc., 1980).

[21]M. L. Von Franz and J. Hillman, *Jung's Typology* (New York: Spring Publications, 1971).

[22]*Metaphysical Bible Dictionary* (Unity Village, Mo.: Unity School of Christianity, 1931).

[23]Malcolm Westcott, *Toward a Contemporary Psychology of Intuition* (New York: Holt, Rinehart, and Winston, 1968), p. 11.

[24]*Foundations of Tibetan Mysticism* (New York: Samuel Weiser, 1969), p. 74.

[25]Robert Assagioli, "Self-Realization and Psychological Disturbances," *Mandalama* (August, 1981), pp. 4–11.

[26]Dan Dorfman, "Alert! They Say What's Hot Is Not," *Chicago-Tribune-New York News Syndicate, Inc.,* 1981. Reprinted by permission: Tribune Company Syndicate, Inc.

[27]"Businesses Integrate Intuitive, Analytical Thinking," *Leading Edge Bulletin* (March 16, 1981), p. 1. Excerpted from *Leading Edge Bulletin,* published by Interface Press, Box 42247, Los Angeles, CA 40042. Used with permission.

[28]Sam Bittner, "Liberal-Arts Majors Prove Specialization Isn't Required for Success in Business," *The Chronicle of Higher Education* (April 14, 1982), p. 25. Reprinted with permission of *The Chronicle of Higher Education,* copyright © 1982 and Sam Bittner, author.

[29]Quoted by Mortimer R. Feinberg and Aaron Levenstein, *op. cit.*

[30]Ibid.

[31]William V. McGinnis, "Decision-Making Process," *Public Management* (February, 1983), p. 17. Copyright © 1983 by International City Management Association. Reprinted with permission of *Public Management* and The International City Management Association.

[32]This treatment on levels of intuitive awareness is discussed in detail in Frances E. Vaughan, *op. cit.*

[33]Tony Bastick, *Intuition: How We Think and Act* (New York: John Wiley & Sons, 1982).

[34]"Two Houston Psychologists Are Proving the Best Defense Is Picking a Good Jury," reprinted/condensed from February 21, 1983 *People Weekly,* Anne Maier, copyright © 1983 Time, Inc.

[35]Feinberg and Levenstein, *op. cit.*

[36]Quoted in *Leading Edge Bulletin* (Los Angeles, Calif.: Interface Press, Inc., September 27, 1982),

p. 4. Excerpted from *Leading Edge Bulletin,* published by Interface Press, Box 42247, Los Angeles, Calif. 40072. Used with permission.

[37]Quoted in *Leading Edge Bulletin* (Los Angeles, Calif.: Interface Press, Inc., December 20, 1982). p. 2. Excerpted from *Leading Edge Bulletin,* published by Interface Press, Box 42247, Los Angeles, Calif. 40042. Used with permission.

[38]Isabel Briggs Myers, *Introduction to Type* (Palo Alto, Calif.: Consulting Psychologists Press, Inc., 1980).

[39]Tony Bastick, *op. cit.*

[40]Isabel Briggs Myers, *The Myers Briggs Type Indicator: Manual 1962* (Palo Alto, Calif.: Consulting Psychologists Press, 1962). Also see the publications and research on the MBTI instrument published by Center for Applications of Psychological Type, Inc., Gainsville, Florida.

[41]Will Schutz, *FIRO Awareness Scales Manual* (Palo Alto, Calif.: Consulting Psychologists Press, 1978).

[42]David Keirsey and Marilyn Bates, *Please Understand Me: An Essay on Temperament Styles* (Del Mar, Calif.: Prometheus Nemesis Books, 1978).

[43]Stephen A. Schwartz and Rand DeMattei, "Mobius Psi-Q Test," *Omni Magazine* (October, 1981). This test was developed with the assistance of E. Torrance at the University of Georgia. Several of the questions in the test are from *Human Information Processing*™ *Survey* authored by William Taggart and E. Paul Torrance (Bensenville, Illinois: Scholastic Testing Service, Inc., 1983).

[44]The first test is cited in footnote 43. The second test, Psi-Q Test II, was published by Stephen A. Schwartz and Rand DeMattei, "Psi-Q Test II: Remote Viewing," *Omni Magazine* (October, 1982).

[45]David Loye, "The 1983 Knowable Future Study," (Carmel, Calif.: Institute For Future Forecasting, 1983).

CHAPTER 2

[1]Stephen A. Schwartz and Rand DeMattei, "Mobius Psi-Q Test," *Omni Magazine* (October, 1981). The questions selected from this test were originally developed by E. Paul Torrance, and appear in William Taggart and E. Paul Torrance, *Human Information Processing*™ *Survey* (Bensenville, Illinois: Scholastic Testing Service, Inc., 1983).

[2]Katharine C. Briggs and Isabel Briggs Myers, *Myers-Briggs Type Indicator: Form F* (Palo Alto, Calif.: Consulting Psychologists Press, 1943 through 1976).

[3]The Mobius Psi-Q Test has been administered nationally to over 15,000 people. For a discussion of the test and findings, see "Psi-Q I Report," *Omni Magazine* (November, 1982), pp. 24 and 160–161. For a discussion of reliability and validity tests on the Myers-Briggs Indicator, see Isabel Briggs Myers, *The Myers-Briggs Type Indicator: Manual* (Palo Alto, Calif.: Consulting Psychologists Press, 1962).

[4]You will note that for the purposes of this test, I have used the term *thinking* as opposed to *sensing* which is the term used in the Myers-Briggs Type Indicator. The reason is that during my pretesting I found that the term *thinking* was clearer to managers than the term *sensing* to depict analytical and deductive processes. Since I was not using the other dimensions of the MBTI here, it did not cause confusion to make this change in terms.

[5]Private sector CEO's were made up of a sample of 88 top executives who were members of the Greater Miami Chamber of Commerce in Florida. Ray Goode, president of The Babcock Company in Coral Gables, Florida and former Dade county manager, wrote a cover letter endorsing the questionnaire and mailed the test out of his office over his letterhead. All the community college presidents in California were mailed the test in that state over Dan Angel's signature, president of the Citrus Community College in Azusa, California, and former state legislator in Michigan. Neil E. Allgood, brigadier general and director, California Specialized Training Institute in San Luis Obispo, California, administered the test personally to his 40th Infantry Division emergency management staff. David Pingree, secretary of the Florida State Department of Health and Rehabilitative Services in Tallahassee, Florida, mailed the test out of his office with a cover letter of support to 110 of his managers statewide. Robert Donly, president of the Florida League of Cities in 1982, also wrote a cover letter explaining the test that was mailed to city

managers in Florida statewide. State legislators and staff were tested in Michigan with the assistance of Senator Robert Vander Laan, former State Senate majority leader, who I served as executive assistant in 1973–74. In addition, the ASPA meeting attendees of Orange and Los Angeles counties were tested in the spring of 1982.

Together, nearly 800 executives were mailed questionnaires besides the national random sample of the ASPA profession. The national ASPA mailing was endorsed with a joint cover letter by three national council members—Gus Turnbull, III (who is also a member of the Board of Editors of *The Public Administration Review*), Jerry O'Neil, and Carolyn B. Lawrence.

[6]The statistical test, One-Way Anova, was used to measure significance. The standard of 0.05 or better was established for rejecting the null hypothesis. That is, the chances of obtaining the differences in scores noted was 5 times in 100 or less. The procedure was applied both horizontally and vertically. That is, scores between management levels, and by management level within each occupational specialization were compared vertically. Similarly, scores horizontally were compared between sexes, ethnic groups, and by occupational specialization. The dominant score on each scale was used for this comparison. For a discussion of how this procedure is conducted, see Lyman Ott and David K. Hildebrand, *Statistical Thinking for Managers* (Boston, Mass.: Duxbury Press, 1983).

[7]"People With Balanced Brains Better Forecasters," *Leading Edge Bulletin*, (vol. 7, no. 3, January 4, 1982), p. 1. Excerpted from *Leading Edge Bulletin*, published by Interface Press, Box 42247, Los Angeles, Calif. Used with permission.

[8]Donald A. Schon, *The Reflective Practitioner: How Professionals Think in Action* (New York: Basic Books, Inc., 1983), p. 239. Reprinted with permission of Basic Books, Inc.

[9]Alice G. Sargent, *The Androgynous Manager* (New York: AMACOM, 1981).

[10]Pamela Weintraub, "The Brain: His and Hers," *Discover Magazine* (April, 1981), pp. 15–20.

[11]Available research thus far does seem to indicate that personality types vary significantly by occupational specialization. See Isabel Briggs Myers and Peter B. Myers, *Gifts Differing* (Palo Alto, Calif.: Consulting Psychologists Press, 1980), particularly Chapter 14 on occupations and types.

[12]Harlan Cleveland, former president of The University of Hawaii, has noted that top managers will need to demonstrate intuitive skills increasingly in the future. Listen to Harlan Cleveland, "Frontiers of Public Administration," address at the National Convention of the American Society for Public Administration (Honolulu, Hawaii: Crown Duplication Tapes, 1982).

[13]Richard Tanner Pascale and Anthony G. Athos, *The Art of Japanese Management: Application for American Executives* (New York: Warner Books, Inc., 1981), especially Chapter 4 on Zen and the art of management.

[14]For practical suggestions on how this process can be carried out, see Gordon Lawrence, *People Types & Tiger Stripes: A Practical Guide to Learning Styles,* 2d ed., (Gainesville, Fla.: Center for Applications of Psychological Type, Inc., 1982).

CHAPTER 3

[1]John Naisbitt, Alvin Toffler, and Willis W. Harman among others have identified these trends outlined in Chapter 1. Also see the regular monthly publication of *The Leading Edge Bulletin* (Los Angeles, Calif.: Interface Press, Inc.).

[2]Kathryn Harris, "Disney Lays the Groundwork for Its Voyage to Tomorrowland," *Los Angeles Times* (June 27, 1982), p. 1 of Business Section.

[3]Personal Interview During Intuitive Workshop (El Paso, Tex., March 4, 1983).

[4]Ibid.

[5]Letter from a woman Ph.D., Management and Organizational Development Advisor, Rockwell International, March 16, 1982.

[6]The instruments cited here have already been referred to and footnoted in Chapters 2 and 3.

[7]One of the most commonly known methods is the *Lozanov Learning Method* for new language learning.

[8]See Joyce Lee, "You Can Raise Your IQ, Increase Your Self-Esteem, Create Energy, Improve Your Memory, and Much, Much More—With Graphotherapy: How Does It Work?" *New Woman Mag-*

azine (July, 1982), pp. 20–24. Also see Charlotte P. Leibel, *Change Your Handwriting Change Your Life* (New York: Stein and Day, 1972).

[9]Practically, it would appear that the whole Walt Disney organization could presently benefit from a BMS intervention to help turn around their profit record on the movie side of the business. For example, see R. Foster Winans, "Disney Stock Falls Something Wicked as Film Opens and Box Office Turns Into Horror Show," *The Wall Street Journal* (May 11, 1983), p. 51. Another current example is Polaroid, where the recent sales decline appears to be linked to the organization's failure to develop a continuing flow of creativity that characterized Edwin Land himself. See Mitchell Lynch, "Polaroid Tries to Get Itself in Focus," *The New York Times* (May 15, 1983), Section F, p. 4.

[10]William Ascher, *Forecasting: An Appraisal for Policy-Makers and Planners* (Baltimore: Johns Hopkins Press, 1978), p. 184; and David Loye, *The Knowable Future: A Psychology of Forecasting and Prophecy* (New York: John Wiley & Sons, 1978).

[11]David Keirsey and Marilyn Bates, *Please Understand Me: An Essay On Temperament Styles* (Del Mar, Calif.: Prometheus Nemesis Books, 1978), p. 175. Reprinted by permission of Prometheus Nemesis Books. For other research on the relationship between MBTI test results, occupational preferences, and success, see *Resources From CAPT* (Gainseville, Fla.: Center for Applications of Psychological Type, May, 1983).

[12]Isabel Briggs Myers and Peter B. Myers, *Gifts Differing* (Palo Alto, Calif.: Consulting Psychologists Press, Inc., 1980), p. 166.

[13]Ibid.

[14]Ibid., Chapter 14. Reprinted by permission of the publisher, Consulting Psychologists Press, Inc., Palo Alto, California 94306 from *Gifts Differing* by Isabel Briggs Myers, copyright © 1980. Further reproduction is prohibited without the publisher's consent.

[15]John Holusha, "Toyota on GM Deal: Giving Aid to Opponent," *The New York Times* (March 17, 1983), p. 1 of Business Section.

[16]Isabel Briggs Myers and Peter B. Myers, op. cit., p. 208. Reprinted by permission of the publisher, Consulting Psychologists Press, Inc. Palo Alto, California 94306 from *Gifts Differing* by Isabel Briggs Myers, copyright © 1980. Further reproduction is prohibited without the publisher's consent.

[17]William S. Howell, *The Emphatic Communicator* (Belmont, Calif.: Wodsworth Publishing Co., 1982), p. 231.

[18]Hughes Aircraft Company: *Employee Opinion Survey* (Philadelphia, Pa.: Hay Associates, 1981).

[19]Carl Sagan, *The Dragons of Eden* (New York: Random House, 1977), p. 181. Reprinted by permission of Random House, Inc.

[20]J. Clayton Lafferty and Alonzo W. Pond, *The Desert Survival Situation: A Group Decision Making Experience for Examining and Increasing Individual and Team Effectiveness* (Plymouth, Mich.: Human Synergistics, 1974).

CHAPTER 4

[1]Cited in the brochure of Psychic Enterprises, Inc., Los Angeles, California.

[2]Cognitive orientations refer to your factual knowledge about a subject. Affective orientation refers to how you feel about a subject—positive or negative. You can have very strong feelings about a subject about which you know very little. Evaluational orientations refers to what you decide to act on based on the product of your cognitive knowledge and affective feelings about a subject. What is important here is the interplay between facts and their impact on your feelings about a subject and vice versa.

[3]Beverly Stephen, "Search Aims for Secrets of Success," (Tribune Company Syndicate, 1982).

[4]Research has shown that one's own skepticism influences ESP scores. Also personality is a factor. Cold and rigid personalities (more likely to be left brain in management style) tend to block the ability they may have. For a discussion of this issue, see Alan Vaughan, "The Time Disbeliever," *Reincarnation Report* (March, 1983), pp. 10–11 and 45.

[5]Letters to the author on May 18, 1982 and June 3, 1982, from Thomas H. Bush, deputy director, Department of the Treasury, State of New Jersey, Trenton, N.J. Reprinted with permission.

[6]Letter to the author on March 19, 1983, from Harry W. Anderson, president of Tri-State Wholesale Associated Grocers, Inc. Reprinted with permission.

⁷Press release of Alan Vaughan. The floppy disk for this game, entitled Psychic Defender, is available by writing Vaughan, Enterprising Ideas, 111 E. Broadway, Suite 18, Glendale, CA 91205.

⁸Frances E. Vaughan, *Awakening Intuition* (Garden City, N.Y.: Anchor Books, 1979), p. 62.

⁹Stanley R. Dean, M.D., president of the American Association for Social Psychiatry, is doing work in this area. He is also particularly active in efforts to bridge the gap between medical science and psychic research.

¹⁰Roger Von Oech, "The Mind as a Management Tool," *Public Management* (January, 1982), p. 7. Copyright © 1982 by International City Management Association. Reprinted by permission of *Public Management* and The International City Management Association.

¹¹Contained in "Editor's Notes," *Public Management* (February, 1983), back of front cover. Copyright © 1983 by International City Management Association. Reprinted by permission of *Public Management* and The International City Management Association.

¹²Roger Von Oech, op. cit. pp. 7–9.

¹³Ed Everett, "Improving Creativity—One Organization's Approach," *Public Management* (February, 1983), p. 7. Copyright © 1983 by International City Management Association. Reprinted by permission of *Public Management* and The International City Management Association.

¹⁴David F. Brown, "Consciousness in Business," *New Realities* (vol. 1, no. 3, 1977), p. 17. Copyright © 1977, and reprinted by permission of New Realities and by Hawthorne/Stone Real Estate & Investments.

¹⁵Ibid., p. 21. Marshall Thurber, one of the founders of the firm, has since left and gone into business for himself in San Diego.

¹⁶Douglas Dean and John Mihalasky, *Executive ESP* (Englewood Cliffs, N.J.: Prentice-Hall, Inc., 1974).

¹⁷Frances E. Vaughan, op. cit.

¹⁸"Editor's Notes" citation, *Public Management* (February, 1983), back of front cover. Copyright © 1983 by International City Management Association. Reprinted by permission of *Public Management* and The International City Management Association.

¹⁹Cited in Commentary Section of *Public Management* (February, 1983), p. 18. This was a special issue devoted to creativity in the public sector. Copyright © 1983 by International City Management Association. Reprinted by permission of *Public Management* and The International City Management Association.

²⁰Frances E. Vaughan, op. cit., p. 183. Excerpt from *Awakening Intuition* by Frances Vaughan, copyright © 1979 by Frances Vaughan, reprinted by permission of Doubleday & Co., Inc.

²¹J. Clayton Lafferty and Alonzo W. Pond, "The Desert Survival Situation: A Group Decision Making Experience for Examining and Increasing Individual and Team Effectiveness" (Plymouth, Mich.: Human Synergistics, 1974).

²²Letter to the author from George Boyadjieff, president of Varco Intl., Inc., Orange, Calif., dated May 11, 1982. Reprinted with permission.

²³Letter to the author from Leonard A. Goodman, Jr., General Agent for John Hancock dated January 28, 1983. Reprinted with permission.

²⁴Evaluations dated February 1, 1983, and March 3, 1983, conducted by the Center for Professional Development, University of Tex., El Paso, which is located in the College of Business.

²⁵Jerry Carroll, "Over-Achievers Swarm to This Exotic Class: MBA's Who Meditate, Chant, and Read Tarot Cards," *San Francisco Chronicle* (February 17, 1983), p. 46. Copyright © 1983 and reprinted with permission of The San Francisco Chronicle.

²⁶Frances E. Vaughan, op. cit., p. 185. Excerpt from *Awakening Intuition* by Frances Vaughan, copyright © 1979 by Frances Vaughan, reprinted by permission of Doubleday & Co., Inc.

²⁷Cited in Frances E. Vaughan, op. cit., p. 154.

²⁸Letter to the author from Maria Elena Toraño, president of META, Miami, Fla., dated March 15, 1982.

²⁹Letter to the author from Jean Mathison, Associate Regional Director, Area Health Education Center, University of Southern California School of Medicine, Los Angeles, Calif., dated February 24, 1983.

³⁰"An Interview with Joseph McKinney, chairman and CEO, Tyler Corporation" in *Travelhost Prosperity Series*, February 28, 1982. Copyright © 1982, reprinted by permission of Travelhost, Inc.

³¹Ibid.

³²Ibid.

[33]Ibid.

[34]Cited in Commentary Section of *Public Management* (February, 1983), pp. 18–19. Reprinted by permission of *Public Management* and The International City Management Association.

[35]Cited in Commentary Section of *Public Management*, op. cit., p. 17. Reprinted by permission of *Public Management* and The International City Management Association.

[36]Ibid. Reprinted by permission of *Public Management* and The International City Management Association.

[37]Ed Everett, op. cit., p. 7. Reprinted by permission of *Public Management* and The International City Management Association.

[38]Ibid. Reprinted by permission of *Public Management* and The International City Management Association.

[39]Alan Vaughan, "Intuition, Precognition, and the Art of Prediction," *The Futurist* (June, 1982), pp. 9–10. Copyright © 1982, reprinted with the permission of *The Futurist,* published by the World Future Society, 4916 St. Elme Ave., Washington, D.C. 20014.

[40]Please refer to the annotated bibliography for further information on this section of the chapter.

[41]Cited in their promotion literature, Human Synergistics, Plymouth, Mich.

[42]Schutz has now refined and expanded the FIRO-B instrument into new measures. See *The Schutz Measures: An Integrated System for Assessing Elements of Awareness* (San Diego, Calif.: University Associates, Inc., 1982).

[43]See Isabel Briggs Myers and Peter B. Myers, op. cit., Chapter 14; and Will Schutz, *FIRO Awareness Scales Manual* (Palo Alto, Calif.: Consulting Psychologists Press, Inc., 1978), p. 10.

CHAPTER 5

[1]Ralph Z. Sorenson, "A Lifetime of Learning to Manage Effectively," *The New York Times* (February 28, 1983), p. 30. © 1983 The New York Times Company. Reprinted by permission.

[2]Ibid.

[3]L. Erik Calonius, "Factory Magic: In a Plant in Memphis, Japanese Firm Shows How to Attain Quality," *The Wall Street Journal* (April 29, 1983), p. 1.

[4]Cited by Bennett W. Goodspeed in "Different Style of Analysis Imperative to Business: More Often Than Not, Intuition, Not Numbers, Tells the Real Story," *American Banker* (November 9, 1981), p. 3. © 1981, reprinted by permission of *American Banker.*

[5]"Harvard's Bok Urges Changing 'Expensive, Inefficient' Legal System, Seeks Law School Curriculum Reform," *The Chronicle of Higher Education* (May 4, 1983), p. 9. Reprinted with permission of *The Chronicle of Higher Education,* copyright © 1983.

[6]Frank Rose, "The Mass Production of Engineers: The Future is Being Designed by Engineers. The One Thing We Know About the Future is That It's More Complicated Than That," *Esquire Magazine* (May, 1983), pp. 74–84. Reprinted by permission of Virginia Barber Literary Agency, Inc., agent for author.

[7]"Visions: Report on Cal State's Future Raises Doubts," *Los Angeles Times* (February 6, 1983), p. 22. Copyright © 1983 Los Angeles Times. Reprinted by permission.

[8]Thomas C. Hayes, "Celestial Seasonings Pins Its Hopes on More Than Herbal Tea," *The New York Times* (April 3, 1983), p. 6. © 1983 The New York Times Company. Reprinted by permission.

[9]Ibid.

[10]"Control Data Enables Its Employees to Redefine Company Values, Destiny," *Leading Edge Bulletin* (February 21, 1983), p. 1. Excerpted from *Leading Edge Bulletin,* published by Interface Press, Box 42247, Los Angeles, CA. Used with permission.

[11]Ibid.

[12]"Going For It: Who Are Today's New Magnates, New Moguls, New Wheeler-Dealers, New Builders of Business Empires: Well, They're Women," *Southwest Airline Magazine* (June, 1983), beginning on p. 75 © 1983, reprinted by permission of Southwest Airlines Magazine.

[13]Stephan A. Schwartz, *The Alexandria Project* (New York: Delacorte; Friede, 1983).

[14]Stephan A. Schwartz and Rand DeMattei, "Mobius Psi-Q Test," *Omni Magazine* (October, 1981).

[15]Stephan A. Schwartz and Rand DeMattei, "Psi-Q I Report," *Omni Magazine* (November, 1982), pp. 160–61. Also author's personal interview with Schwartz in November, 1981, in Los Angeles, Calif.

[16]Ibid.

[17]Stephan A. Schwartz and Rand DeMattei, "Psi-Q Test II: Remote Viewing," *Omni Magazine* (October, 1982), pp. 134–143.

[18]"Psi-Q II Feedback Report" (Los Angeles, Calif.: The Mobius Group, 1982).

[19]Cited in Stephan A. Schwartz and Rand DeMattei, "Psi-Q I Report," op. cit., p. 161.

[20]If you wish to review a few independent evaluations of the projections based on left brain techniques, see for example Louise McGinley, "Forecasters Overhaul 'Models' of Economy in Wake of 1982 Errors," *The Wall Street Journal* (February 17, 1983), p. 1.

[21]"The 1983 Knowable Future Study" (Carmel, Calif.: Institute for Futures Forecasting, 1983).

[22]Alan Vaughan, "Intuition, Precognition, and the Art of Prediction," *The Futurist* (June, 1982), p. 10. Copyright © 1982 reprinted with the permission of The Futurist, published by the World Future Society, 4916 St. Elmo Ave., Washington, D.C. 200140.

[23]"People with 'Balanced Brains' Better Forecasters," *Brain-Mind Bulletin* (January 4, 1982), p. 1.

[24]David Loye, "Foresight Saga," *Omni Magazine* (September, 1982), p. 134. See also Douglas Colligan, "Your Gift of Prophecy," *Reader's Digest* (September, 1982), pp. 145–149.

[25]Alfred L. Malabre, Jr., "If One Economist Goofs, Will 46 Do Any Better? Robert Eggert Thinks So, and He May Be Right," *The Wall Street Journal* (April 6, 1983), p. 50.

[26]Ibid.

[27]"Training Intuition with 'The Psychic Defender'," press release of Alan Vaughan (Glendale, Calif., 1983).

[28]"Inferential Focus: Business Inferential Scanning" (New York: Inferential Focus, 1981).

[29]Dan Dorfman, "Alert! They Say What's Hot is Not," *Chicago Tribune-New York News Syndicate* (1981), p. 35. Reprinted by permission: Tribune Company Syndicate, Inc.

[30]Cited in Bennett W. Goodspeed, op. cit., p. 3. © 1981, reprinted by permission of *American Banker*.

[31]Weston H. Agor, "Using Intuition in Public Management, *Public Management* (February, 1983), pp. 2–6. For other articles of mine on this subject, see Weston H. Agor, "Brain Skills Development in Management Training," *Training and Development Journal* (April, 1983), pp. 78–83; Weston H. Agor, "Training Public Managers to Develop and Use Their Intuition for Decision Making" in Kent T. Higgins, ed., *Professional Development Handbook* (Washington, D.C.: American Society for Public Administration, 1983), pp. 1–6; Weston H. Agor, "Tomorrow's Intuitive Leaders," *The Futurist* (August, 1983) pp. 49–53, copyright © 1983, reprinted with the permission of *The Futurist*, published by The World Future Society, 4916 St. Elmo Ave., Washington, D.C. 20014. and Weston H. Agor, "Management in the Future: Using Intuitive Thinking," *Real Estate Business* (Summer, 1983), pp. 14–17 and 27.

[32]Roger Von Oech, "The Mind as a Management Tool," *Public Management* (January, 1982), pp. 7–9; and Marilyn Grey, "Creative Thinking," *Public Management* (February, 1983), pp. 10– and 14–15. Copyright © 1982, 1983 by International City Management Association. Reprinted by permission of *Public Management* and the International City Management Association.

[33]Willis W. Harman, "This 20 Year Present," *Public Management* (January-February, 1980), p. 7. Copyright © 1980 by International City Management Association. Reprinted by permission of *Public Management* and The International City Management Association.

[34]"A New Source for Business Success" (Los Angeles, Calif.: Psychic Enterprises, Inc., 1983).

[35]Philip Goldberg, *The Intuitive Edge* (Los Angeles, Calif.: J. P. Tarcher, Inc., 1983).

[36]Jerry Carroll, "Over-Achievers Swarm to This Exotic Class: MBAs Who Meditate, Chant, and Read Tarot Cards," *San Francisco Chronicle* (February 17, 1983), p. 46. Also see Eric N. Berg, "Zen and the Stanford Business Student," *New York Times* (January 30, 1983), p. 9.

[37]Ibid. © 1983 *San Francisco Chronicle*. Used with permission.

[38]"System Dynamics Aids Intuition," *Leading Edge Bulletin* (April 26, 1982), p. 1. Excerpted from *Leading Edge Bulletin*, published by Interface Press, Box 42247, Los Angeles, CA 40042. Used with permission.

[39]Ibid., p. 2.

[40]Materials provided to author by Martin Krasney, president, American Leadership Forum in letter dated February 15, 1983.

[41]See for example Ena Naunton, "Brain Wars: Which Side Are You On? The Right Side Just Might be a Life Saver," *Miami Herald* (February 20, 1983, Section G), pp. 1 and 8; and "Top Managers Use More

Intuitive Skills, Study Says," *Leading Edge Bulletin* (February 21, 1983), pp. 1 and 2. Workshops have been run from coast to coast and abroad in 1983 with major presentations in Los Angeles at The University of Southern California and the American Society for Training and Development Organizational Development "New Horizons Conference" in Phoenix for Arizona State University, and in Latin America. For a treatment of my Latin American workshops, see Maria Elena Baradat De Valle, "La Intuicion: Explorando El Sexto Sentido," *Harpers Bazaar En Español* (June, 1983), pp. 70–71 and 103.

Annotated Bibliography

So, you have decided you want to measure and develop your intuitive ability further; you would like to be able to use this skill to make decisions on the job more productively. Below is a selected list of annotated resources so that you can pick and choose items *you feel* will be most helpful to you. The list of resources is organized by subject following the basic outline of this book:

- What is intuition?
- Test and measurement of intuition.
- Practical use of intuition in management.
- How to develop your intuitive ability.
- Innovative use of intuition in modern organizations.

1. WHAT IS INTUITION?

For purposes of organizing this section, we are using Francis E. Vaughan's definition of intuition, "It is a way of knowing . . . recognizing the possibilities in any situation. Extrasensory perception, clairvoyance, and telepathy are part of the intuitive function."

Books

AGEE, DORIS. *Edgar Cayce on ESP*. New York: Warner Books, 1969. Describes the varieties of intuition that can be found in the records of Edgar Cayce's work. Cayce, now deceased, was a famous and gifted psychic who often used his powers to find health cures for clients when traditional medicine appeared to fail.

BASTICK, TONY. *Intuition: How We Think and Act.* New York: John Wiley & Sons, 1982. Highly technical but also valuable approach to the subject. This book is an effort to build a scientific theory of intuition that can be used to guide research. Summarizes most recent research on the topic.

BERNE, ERIC. *Intuition and Ego States.* San Francisco, Calif.: T. A. Press, 1977. Compilation of papers on the topic by the author of *Games People Play* that later leads to his approach to psychotherapy called *transactional analysis.*

CAYCE, HUGH LYNN. *Venture Inward: The Incredible Story of Edgar Cayce.* New York: Harper & Row, Inc., 1964. Guide to opening intuition beyond consciousness, the ways such insight can be achieved, and the dangers of some.

DEAN, DOUGLAS, et. al. *Executive ESP.* Englewood Cliffs, N.J.: Prentice-Hall, Inc., 1974. Discusses test and results of work with chief executive officers that showed those who had precognitive ability also had the highest profit record.

Editors of *Psychic, Psychics: In-Depth Interviews.* New York: Harper & Row, Inc., 1972. Interviews by the editors of the now-defunct magazine called *Psychic,* that has been renamed *New Realities.*

FISHER, MILTON. *Intuition: How to Use It for Success and Happiness.* New York: E. P. Dutton, 1981. Popularized introduction to the subject. Reading list may be of interest to you.

GIBSON, SANDRA. *Beyond the Body.* New York: Tower Publications, Inc., 1979. Story of a young woman who discovered she possessed psychic powers as chroniclized from her journal. The technique used to unblock her was hypnotherapy.

GOLDBERG, PHILIP. *The Intuitive Edge.* Los Angeles, Calif.: J. P. Tarcher, Inc., 1983. Treats the broad subject of how an intuitive person thinks. Contains a how-to-develop-the-skill section.

KARAGULLA, SHAFICA. *Breakthrough to Creativity: Your Higher Sense Perception.* Marina Del Rey, Calif.: De Vorss & Co., Inc., 1967. Eight years of research with "sensitives' " ability to use intuition in a variety of ways.

OSTRANDER, SHEILA and SCHROEDER, LYNN. *Psychic Discoveries Behind the Iron Curtain.* New York: Bantam Books, Inc., 1970. Reports on the research concerning ESP (one intuitive skill) behind the iron curtain.

PROGOFF, IRA. *Jung, Synchronicity, and Human Destiny: Noncausal Dimensions of Human Experience.* New York: Delta Publishing Co., Inc., 1973. Discusses the famous psychologist Carl Jung's late-in-life work on synchronicity that is "when two or more events, each with its own causality, come together for no apparent reason to produce an important result."

ROBBINS, SHAWN. *Ahead of Myself: Confessions of a Professional Psychic.* Englewood Cliffs, N.J.: Prentice-Hall, Inc., 1980. Personal experiences of a professional psychic, and how she learned to deal with her gifts, with suggestions for you, too.

TARGG, RUSSELL and PUTOFF, HAROLD. *Mind-Research: Scientists Look at Psychic Ability.* New York: Dell Publishing Co., Inc., 1977. Discusses experiments examined by two physicists that involved the intuitive skills, ESP, and remote viewing.

VAUGHAN, FRANCES E. *Awakening Intuition.* Garden City, N.Y.: Anchor Books, 1979. Written by a transpersonal psychologist. Probably the best book currently available on what it is, and how to develop it. Her appendix, "Guidelines for Awakening Intuition," is a jewel.

Articles

ASSAGIOLI, ROBERTO. "Self-Realization and Psychological Disturbances." *Mandalama Journal* (August, 1981), pp. 4–11. Discusses the steps to superconsciousness and the experiences that help you to know you are both on your way and also okay.

BROWDER, SUE. "Women's Intuition: Our Formidable Advantage." *Cosmopolitan Magazine* (April, 1983), pp. 235–237. Discusses the topic in popularized manner with test included.

HARMAN, WILLIS W. "Creative/Intuitive Decision Making: A New Thrust for Ions." *Institute of Noetic Sciences Newsletter* (no date), pp. 1 and 20–22. Discusses efforts to research the topic that, apparently, has not been funded at the Institute since the article was published.

HERRMANN, NED. "The Creative Brain." Mimeographed unpublished. Discusses the work he has done in workshops to change brain styles.

JASTROW, ROBERT. "Mind Gates." *Science Digest* (November, 1981). Attempts to explain processes such as creativity, pride, and joy in terms of simple, logical steps that underlie all computers.

PRINCE, GEORGE. "Creativity and Learning Skills, Not Talents." *The Phillips Exeter Bulletin* (June-July and September-October, 1980), reprint. Explains the difference between left brain and right brain thinking styles and skills. Useful as a general background so that you can see where the intuitive function can fit in your overall thinking patterns.

ROBBINS, SHAWN. "Those Subtle Little Voices Within." *New Woman Magazine* (October, 1982), pp. 64–68. Section on how to develop your intuition from her book cited above.

SPERRY, ROGER. "Some Effects of Disconnecting the Cerebral Hemispheres." Nobel Lecture, December 8, 1981. Lecture by the Nobel Prize winner on this split brain research that became popularized as left brain and right brain thinking. Recently this work is being questioned as being oversimplified. It is questionable that all of our intuitive insights simply come from only one area of the brain.

"The Spring Hill Education Conference Issue." *Institute of Noetic Sciences Newsletter* (Spring, 1982). Covers treatment of conference on exploration concerning the untapped potential we have in the total field of intuition.

"The Two Sides of the Brain." *Science* (April, 1983), pp. 488–490. Summarizes recent research on behavioral asymmetries and their link to physical asymmetries in the brain.

VAUGHAN, FRANCIS E. "What Is Intuition?" *New Realities* (Spring, 1982), pp. 16–22. Essentially a summary of her book above, along with quotes from people who use intuition in various walks of life.

WEINTRAUB, PAMELA. "The Brain: His and Hers." *Discover* (April, 1981), pp. 15–20. Discusses research suggesting that if men and women do think differently, it may be linked to brain development physically.

2. TEST AND MEASUREMENT OF INTUITION

There are a number of tests and instruments that can be used to measure intuition as defined above. Some are more traditionally recognized methods, while others are less formally recognized. Examples of both are cited for your own review and consideration.

Books and Monographs

BRENNER, ELIZABETH. *Hand in Hand: Awareness and Compatibility—It's in Your Hands.* Millbrae, Calif.: Celestial Arts, 1981. Characteristics derived by professional palm reading.

EBON, MARTIN, ed. *Test Your ESP.* New York: New American Library, Inc., 1970. Real life tests and exercises to measure this aspect of your intuitive ability.

LEIBEL, CHARLOTTE P. *Change Your Handwriting, Change Your Life.* New York: Stein and Day, 1972. Explains how handwriting can be used to test your intuitive ability, as well as other characteristics, and to change yourself as well. See particularly the chapter on intuition and imagination. Because this person also has a strong formal training in the fields of law and psychology, her own capability of interpretation shows how this approach can be effectively used.

LOYE, DAVID. *The Knowable Future: A Psychology of Forecasting and Prophecy.* New York: John Wiley & Sons, 1978. Test measures are included and described for measuring precognitive ability.

MYERS, ISABEL BRIGGS. *Introduction to Type.* Palo Alto, Calif.: Consulting Psychologists Press, Inc., 1980. Explains characteristics and likely behavior based on your type after taking the Myers-Briggs Personality Test. The section on intuition is particularly useful, but so are other descriptions.

MYERS, ISABEL BRIGGS. *The Myers-Briggs Type Indicator: 1962 Manual.* Palo Alto, Calif.: Consulting Psychologists Press, 1962. Explains the Myers-Briggs Type Indicator, how it works, and how it can be interpreted, as well as other statistical support information, on its use by organizations.

TAGGART, WILLIAM. *Administrators Manual for the Human Information Processing™ Survey and Strategy and Tactics Profiles.* Bensenville, Illinois: Scholastic Testing Service, Inc. 1983. Describes how to interpret and use the results of the Human Information™ Survey. Also discusses the reliability and validity of the survey instrument.

Articles

AGOR, WESTON H. "Brain Skills Development in Management Training." *Training and Development Journal* (April, 1983), pp. 78–83. Describes test and findings that measured intuitive ability, as well as brain styles, on the job.

BUNDERSON, C. V. and HERRMANN, W. E. "Patterns of Brain Dominance and Their Relationship to Tests of Cognitive Processing, Personality, and Learning Style." Mimeographed, (no date). Discusses tests and findings in an attempt to identify a battery of personal profile measures that could be useful in educational and instructional settings.

LEE, JOYCE. "You Can Raise Your IQ, Increase Your Self-Esteem, Create Energy, Improve Your Memory and Much Much More—with Graphotherapy." *New Woman Magazine* (July, 1982), pp. 20–24. Discussed in popularized form, Charlotte Leibel's book contents above.

LOYE, DAVID. "Foresight Saga." *Omni Magazine* (September, 1982), pp. 20–134. Summarizes his research as outlined in the book above.

SCHKADE, LAWRENCE L. and POTVIN, ALFRED R. "Cognitive Style, EEG Waveforms, and Brain Levels." *Human Systems Management Journal* (1981), pp. 329–331. Uses Herrmann Learning Profile Survey Form and applies EEG tests to selected subjects. Finds that it validates the Herrmann test.

SCHWARTZ, STEPHAN A. and DeMATTEI, RAND. "Psi-Q I Report." *Omni Magazine* (November, 1982), pp. 24 and 160–161. Summarizes the results of their national testing of over 18,000 *Omni Magazine* readers who took their test that measures precognitive ability as well as brain styles in 1981–82.

"The Eyes Have It When Interviewing Suspects," *Public Administration Times* (April 15, 1983), p. 12. Research of Dr. Dale G. Leathers at The University of Georgia shows which nonverbal cues mean what as contrasted with actual verbal statements being made by a respondent.

"Two Houston Psychologists Are Proving the Best Defense is Picking a Good Jury." *People Magazine* (February, 1983), pp. 88–90. Intuition is used to pick juries.

TUCKER, CARLL. "I Got My Job Through Human Engineering." *The Village Voice* (November 3, 1975), reprint. Describes aptitude measurement program by The Johnson O'Connor Research Foundation.

VIVIAN, ELEANOR L. "Personality Can be 'Seen' in Graphic Evaluation Chart." *The Journal of Graphoanalysis* (January, 1983), p. 7. Describes how graphoanalysis can be professionally used to measure traits and characteristics including intuition.

Test Instruments

AGOR, WESTON H. "Test Your Management Style." (1982). Based on selected questions from the intuition portion of The Myers-Briggs Type Indicator and the brain styles portion of The Mobius Psi-Q I Test Instruments. Measures underlying potential to use intuition as well as gives an indication of whether it is being used on the job to make decisions.

AGOR, WESTON H. "Test Your Management Style Response Form." (1982). Used with above test to graphically tell respondents how they scored and what it means. Also has section where Agor personally writes "whatever he picks up on the individual" intuitively whether he has met the person personally or not.

BRIGGS, KATHARINE C. and BRIGGS MYERS, ISABEL. *Myers-Briggs Type Indicator—Form F*. Palo Alto, Calif.: Consulting Psychologists Press, Inc. (1976). Test that can be used to measure aspects of your personality including intuition. It is considered to be highly reliable and valid in the field of psychology although there are those who believe that pen and pencil tests cannot effectively be used to measure actual expected behavior.

FISHER, MILTON. "How Intuitive Are You?" *New Woman Magazine* (May,

1982), pp. 42–44 and 46. Includes test from Fisher's book above. This is a popularized test instrument and probably should not be used other than for fun as a guide. Rely on the other tests noted here for this purpose.

LOYE, DAVID. "Manual for the HCP Profile Test." Carmel, Calif.: Institute for Futures Forecasting, 1982. Seeks to measure brain styles and relationship to ability to forecast the future.

LOYE, DAVID. "The 1983 Knowable Future Study." Carmel, Calif.: Institute for Futures Forecasting, 1983. Seeks to measure brain styles and relationship to ability to forecast events in the immediate future of 1983.

SCHWARTZ, STEPHAN A. and DEMATTEI, RAND. "Mobius Psi-Q Test." *Omni Magazine* (October, 1981). Contains excellent test of both precognitive ability and also brain styles on the job with stratification for other factors such as sex and occupational specialty.

SCHWARTZ, STEPHAN A. and DEMATTEI, RAND. "Psi-Q Test II: Remote Viewing." *Omni Magazine* (October, 1982). Attempt to measure ability to see distant scenes or events using psychic powers alone. Experimental and innovative work.

TORRANCE, E. PAUL with BARBARA and WILLIAM TAGGART. *Human Information*™ *Survey.* Bensenville, Illinois: Scholastic Testing Service, Inc., 1983. Surveys how a person processes information, and classifies the results into left, right, mixed, and integrated processor. Right processors prefer intuitive approaches to problems and decision making.

Advertisement

"Saab Car: A Car for the Left Side of Your Brain—A Car for the Right Side of Your Brain." *The Wall Street Journal* (January, 1982).

3. PRACTICAL USE OF INTUITION IN MANAGEMENT

Books

ASCHER, WILLIAM. *Forecasting: An Appraisal for Policy-Makers and Planners.* Baltimore, Md.: Johns Hopkins University Press, 1978. Discusses different types of forecasting including the use of intuition as a particular application.

BLUMBERG, STEPHEN K. *Win-Win Administration: How to Manage an Organization So Everybody Wins.* Sun Lakes, Ariz.: Thomas Horton and Daughters, 1983. Example of the move to more cooperative styles of management where intuitive skills will be most useful.

CARSKADON, THOMAS G. (Editor). *Research in Psychological Type: Volumes 5 and 6.* Mississippi State, Mississippi: Mississippi State University, 1982 and 1983. Outlines in a series of articles the practical application of MBTI results to various organizational settings and problems including cross-cultural.

Editors, *Harvard Business Review. On Human Relations.* New York: Harper & Row, Inc., 1979. Focuses on right brain aspects of management including a section on intuitive ways of relating to people.

FERGUSON, MARILYN. *The Aquarian Conspiracy: Personal and Social Transformation in the 1980's.* Los Angeles, Calif.: J. P. Tarcher, Inc., 1980. Shows how right brain intuitive approaches are transforming the way we manage all types of organizations and our personal life as well.

FLORY, CHARLES D. *Managing Through Insight.* New York: Mentor Paperback, 1968. Discusses the practical use of right brain skills in management decision making.

GIRDANO, DANIEL and EVERLY, GEORGE. *Controlling Stress and Tension: A Holistic Approach.* Englewood Cliffs, N.J.: Prentice-Hall, Inc., 1979. Shows how important stress management is and right brain approaches for managing. Learning to follow your intuition will help you to reduce stress and manage better.

HOWELL, WILLIAM S. *The Empathic Communicator.* Belmont, Calif.: Wadsworth Publishing Co., 1982. Discusses the importance of empathy in organizational communication. Several examples of the use and importance of intuition are included.

KEIRSEY, DAVID and BATES, MARILYN. *Please Understand Me: An Essay on Temperament Styles.* Del Mar, Calif.: Promethesus Nemesis Books, 1978. Details how the Myers-Briggs personality types are likely to function in organizational settings and in their personal lives. Very useful to show you how to apply intuition scores to solve practical business problems.

LAWRENCE, GORDON. *People Types and Tiger Stripes: A Practical Guide to Learning Styles, 2d ed.* Gainesville, Fla.: Center for Applications of Psychological Type, Inc., 1982. Takes the Myers-Briggs Personality types, explains different learning styles, and gives exercises on how to alter your type (or develop it). Useful practically to show again how intuition can be used in a variety of organizational settings.

MCCAULLEY, MARY H. *Executive Summary: Application of the Myers-Briggs*

Type Indicator to Medicine and other Health Professions. Gainesville, Florida: Center for Applications of Psychological Type, Inc., 1978. Discusses how the MBTI can be used to guide career selection in the medical and other health professions as well as related matters such as patient care.

McCAULLEY, MARY H. et. al. *Applications of Psychological Type in Engineering Education.* Gainesville, Florida: Center for Applications of Psychological Type, Inc., 1983. Discusses how the MBTI can be used to guide career selection and education in the field of engineering.

MUSASHI, MIYAMOTO. *The Book of Five Rings: The Real Art of Japanese Management.* New York: Bantam Books, 1982. Shows how inductive methods can be used to manage your organization and your life. Clearly intuition is one of those.

MYERS, ISABEL BRIGGS with MYERS, PETER B.. *Gifts Differing.* Palo Alto, Ca.: Consulting Psychologists Press, Inc., 1980. Excellent practical guide on how to use Myers-Briggs Test to address all types of organizational problems. It shows also which occupations intuitive types are most likely to be effective at.

MYERS, ISABEL BRIGGS. *Type and Teamwork.* Gainesville, Florida: Center for Applications of Psychological Type, Inc., 1974. Outlines how MBTI results can be used as a guide for effective team building and management in organizations of all types.

PASCALE, RICHARD TANNER and ATHOS, ANTHONY G. *The Art of Japanese Management: Applications for American Executives.* New York: Warner Books, 1981. Key to inductive approaches and their application to management. Chapter 4 on Zen and the art of management is particularly relevant to showing how intuition can be applied to management settings.

PETERS, THOMAS and WATERMAN, ROBERT. *In Search of Excellence.* New York: Harper & Row, 1983. Tells how America's best run companies function and finds that the traits correlated with those of a creative person are often associated with right and integrative thinking.

SARGENT, ALICE G. *The Androgynous Manager.* New York: AMACOM, 1981. Outlines in many ways how and why top managers need to be both intuitive and integrative to succeed.

SCHON, DONALD A. *The Reflective Practitioners—How Professionals Think in Action.* New York: Basic Books, Inc., 1983. Treats different types of professionals and how they think. The importance and use of intuition is treated frequently.

VOCINO, THOMAS and RABIN, JACK, eds. *Contemporary Public Administration.* New York: Harcourt Brace Jovanovich, Inc., 1981. This basic introduction to public management treats the importance of intuitive decision making and how it compares to the so-called rational and empirical models.

ZAGER, ROBERT and ROSOW, MICHAEL P., *The Innovative Organization: Productivity Programs in Action.* Elmsford, N.Y.: Pergamon Press, Inc., 1982. Shows how employee participation must, and will, increase in organizations if productivity is to be increased. Intuition will become more important as a skill of management in this process.

Articles

AGOR, WESTON H. "Using Intuition in Public Management." *Public Management* (February, 1983), pp. 2–6. Reports on testing of over 2000 managers nationally, and outlines how intuition can be used and trained for in public organizations.

"An Interview with Joseph McKinney: Chairman and CEO, Tyler Corporation." *Travelhost Prosperity Series* (February 28, 1982), pp. 4–5. This executive describes his "stray bullet drills" and use of intuition to make decisions.

BENNIS, WARREN. "Leadership Transforms Vision Into Action." *Industry Week* (May 31, 1982), pp. 54–56. Shows how an integrated-intuitive executive provides leadership.

BITTNER, SAM. "Liberal Arts Majors Prove Specialization Isn't Required for Success in Business." *The Chronicle of Higher Education* (April 14, 1982), p. 25. How intuition can be used to recruit successfully in spite of apparent facts.

BOLEN, JAMES GRAYSON. "Interview: Al Pollard." *Psychic* (December, 1974). Successful businessman tells how he views ESP and uses intuition in business.

BROWN, DAVID F. "Consciousness Can Lead to Profits—Outward & Inward—So Proves H/S, a San Francisco Real Estate Firm." *New Realities* (vol. 1, no. 3, 1977), pp. 17–22. Describes how an organization can succeed with a positive, supportive environment using intuition.

CALONIUS, L. ERIK. "Factory Magic: In a Plant in Memphis, Japanese Firm Shows How to Attain Quality." *The Wall Street Journal* (April 29, 1983), pp. 1 and 14. A supportive and cooperative environment emphasizing inductive as well as deductive techniques is discussed.

CATES, CAMILLE. "Beyond Muddling: Creativity." *Public Administration Review* (November/December, 1979), pp. 527–532. Argues for an integrative approach to management that includes intuition.

DENHARDT, ROBERT E. "Managerial Intuition." *MBA* (February/March,

1979), pp. 13–19. Discusses the importance of intuition in key management decisions.

DOLAN, CARRIE. "A Bit of Old-Style Imagination Leads to a High-Tech Success." *The Wall Street Journal* (February, 1983). Describes how she went from a 29-year-old mother of two to a business with $10 million in sales.

FEINBERG, MORTIMER R. and LEVENSTEIN, AARON. "How Do You Know When to Rely on Your Intuition?" *The Wall Street Journal* (June 21, 1982), p. 16. Gives examples of executive use and hints on how and when to use it.

GOODSPEED, BENNETT W. "Different Style of Analysis Imperative to Business: More Often than Not, Intuition, Not Numbers, Tells the Real Story," *American Banker* (November 9, 1981), Reprint. Partner of Inferential Focus of New York tells why intuition counts and when.

GREY, MARILYN. "Creative Thinking." *Public Management* (February, 1983), pp. 10–15. This psychologist tells the International City Managers Association how to think intuitively and why.

HARMAN, WILLIS W. "This 20-Year Present." *Public Management* (January-February, 1980), pp. 4–7. Explains why intuition will be more important in future management.

HARRIS, KATHRYN. "Disney Lays the Groundwork for Its Voyage to Tomorrowland." *Los Angeles Times*, Business Section (June 27, 1982), p. 1. What happened since the departure of intuitive Walt Disney is explained.

HERRMANN, NED. "The Brain and Management Learning." *The Bureaucrat* (Fall, 1982), pp. 17–21. Describes his whole brain approach to learning and creativity in management.

HOLUSHA, JOHN. "Toyota on G.M. Deal: Giving Aid to Opponent." *The New York Times* (March 17, 1983), pp. 1 and 36. Shows how the East and West view management from the right and left brain perspectives relatively.

LYNCH, MITCHELL. "Polaroid Tries to Get Itself in Focus," *The New York Times* (May 15, 1983), Section F, p. 4. Discusses the problems the company is having generating the level of creativity that characterized the company under the leadership of Edwin Land.

NELSON, BRYCE. "Bosses Face Less Risk Than the Bossed." *The New York Times* (April 3, 1983), p. 9. Indicates how stress and intuition can be linked by occupational specialty and level of responsibility.

NELSON, BRYCE "Management 'Revolution' Urged for Auto Industry." *Los Angeles Times* (July 27, 1982), pp. 1 and 15. Need for a change in business consciousness is discussed based on auto industry experience.

NICHOLS, DAVID A. "Can 'Theory Z' Be Applied to Academic Management?" *The Chronicle of Higher Education* (September 1, 1982), p. 72. Going to the East for answers in our higher education system is his suggestion.

LEAVITT, HAROLD J. "Beyond the Analytical Manager." *California Management Journal* (spring, 1975), pp. 5–12. Talks about the important need for right brain skills like intuition.

LEAVITT, HAROLD J. "Beyond the Analytical Manager: Part II." *California Management Journal* (summer, 1975), pp. 11–21. Continues his above article also with a discussion of ESP and techniques used for getting in touch with this ability.

PRINCE, GEORGE M. "Creative Meetings Through Power Sharing." *Harvard Business Review* (July-August, 1972), pp. 47–54. How cooperation and support can work. Intuition tells you how.

PRINCE, GEORGE M. "Putting the Other Half of the Brain to Work." *Training* (November, 1978), reprint. Tells you how to tap into the right side of the brain.

"Putting Heart Back Into the Business of Business." *Management Practice* (spring, 1977), pp. 1–4. Importance of liking your work and knowing what you like. Intuition certainly won't hurt.

RAUDSEPP, EUGENE. "Trust That Hunch!" *Success* (August, 1982), pp. 27–30. Proposes using intuition—it works.

SIEBERT, AL. "The Survivor Personality." *Portland Oregonian-Northwest Magazine* (January 27, 1980). This is one of the best articles I have seen outlining what it will take for an executive to survive in the balance of this decade. The author includes ESP as one required skill. Highly recommended reading.

SORENSON, RALPH Z. "A Lifetime of Learning to Manage Effectively." *The Wall Street Journal* (February 28, 1983), p. 30. Experienced executive tells what it takes to manage effectively. Being sensitive to differences helps.

STEPHEN, BEVERLY. "Search Aims for Secrets of Success." *Tribune Company Syndicate* (1982). Secrets correlate with characteristics of an intuitive manager.

SUGG, JOHN. "Making the Leap—Successful Entrepreneurs and Executives Trust Their Hunches—and It Pays Off." *Working Women* (November, 1982), pp. 38–42. Successful use of intuition in business is outlined.

SULLIVAN, MICHAEL P. "The Intuitive Approach is Making a Quiet Comeback." *American Banker* (March 16, 1983), p. 4. Banks like intuition these days.

TAGGART, WILLIAM and ROBEY, DANIEL. "Mind and Managers: On the Dual Nature of Human Information Processing and Management." *Academy of Management* (vol. 6, no. 2), pp. 187–195. Styles by occupation are discussed. Artists tend to be intuitive while technicians are thinkers. Urges dual-brain teaching in management educational programs. In the next issue of the same magazine (vol. 6, no. 3), pp. 375–383, in "Measuring Managers' Minds: The Assessment of Style in Human Information Processing," the authors discuss ways of testing for thinking styles among managers.

"The World's Smartest Man Revisited," *Inferential Focus Report* (April 11, 1983). Examines the Soviet Leader Andropov from a right brain perspective. The conclusion—he is left out.

TRAIN, JOHN. "How to Feel: The Tao Theory." *Money & Investments* (IF Reprint, April, 1983). Go with the right brain too.

YOSHIHARA, NANCY. "Japan's Strategies May Need Some Tuning to Work Here," *Los Angeles Times* (January 23, 1983), part V, p. 3. Discusses the Japanese approach to management, the latest books on the subject, and the broader structure in Japan that supports business development such as a government support system. Concludes that some adjustments need to be made in both management and government in this country for Japanese management concepts to work fully here.

4. HOW TO DEVELOP YOUR INTUITIVE ABILITY

Books and Monographs

BRO, HARMON H. *Edgar Cayce on Dreams.* New York: Warner Books, 1968. Through this psychic's eyes, advice on how to use your dreams as a tool to get in touch with your intuition.

EDWARDS, BETTY. *Drawing on the Right Side of the Brain.* Los Angeles, Calif.: J. P Tarcher, 1979. How to draw even if you were never an artist. Tells you how to tap into the right side of the brain to do so. This technique or others like it is one way to develop your intuition. See chapter on Zen in drawing in particular.

DE A'MORELLI, RICHARD. *ESP Party Games: Psychic Tests for Everyone.* Chatsworth, Calif.: Major Books, 1979. Games you can play to work on developing your intuitive ability.

GARDNER, MARTIN. *Aha! Insight.* New York: Scientific American, Inc., 1978. Problems to work on to develop your intuitive skills.

GITTNER, LOUIS. *Listen, Listen, Listen: Opens the Door to Spiritual Transformation.* Orcas Island, Wash.: Louis Foundation, 1980. Type of book to read when you need philosophical food to alter or consider altering your present way of thinking.

HERZOG, STEPHANIE. *Joy in the Classroom.* Boulder Creek, Calif.: University of the Trees Press, 1982. Teaching meditation and other techniques at the primary and secondary school level. I have been to their school and the energy the students have is incredible. I recommend every school district look at what they have to offer.

HILLS, CHRISTOPHER. *Creative Conflict: Learning to Love with Total Honesty.* Boulder Creek, Calif.: University of the Trees Press, 1980. Learning to manage conflict by first getting in touch with yourself.

HILLS, CHRISTOPHER. *Into Meditation Now: A Course on Direct Enlightenment.* Boulder Creek, Calif.: University of the Trees Press, 1979. Introduction to meditation techniques which can be followed up by other materials that they have available for further development.

HILLS, CHRISTOPHER and ROZMAN, DEBORAH. *Exploring Inner Space: Awareness Games for All Ages.* Boulder Creek, Calif.: University of the Trees Press, 1978. How to get in touch with your own self and, thereby, everyone else.

HILLS, NORAH. *You Are a Rainbow.* Boulder Creek, Calif.: University of the Trees Press, 1979. Discusses aura levels and aura balancing.

HOUSTON, JEAN. *The Possible Human: A Course in Enhancing Your Physical, Mental, and Creative Abilities.* Los Angeles, Calif.: J. P. Tarcher, Inc., 1982. Teaches you some of the ways to get in touch with yourself and your intuitive ability.

JAMPOLSKY, GERALD G. *Love is Letting Go of Fear.* New York: Bantam Books, Inc., 1981. One of the keys to developing your intuition is developing the capacity to give up the past when necessary. This tells you how.

JOY, W. BRUGH. *Joy's Way: A Map for the Transformational Journey.* Los Angeles, Calif.: J. P. Tarcher, Inc., 1979. Tells you how to develop your Psi ability based on his experience as a doctor.

KRIEGER, DOLORES. *The Therapeutic Touch: How to Use Your Hands to Help or to Heal.* Englewood Cliffs, N.J.: Prentice-Hall, Inc., 1979. A nurse, who has taught how we can heal ourselves and others, tells you how here.

LITVAK, STUART B. *Use Your Head: How to Develop the Other 80% of Your Brain.* Englewood Cliffs, N.J.: Prentice-Hall, Inc., 1982. Very useful book to help you get in touch with your real potential. Chapter on intuition is a good introduction. This might be a book to start with.

MANNING, AL G. *Helping Yourself with E.S.P.* West Nyack, N.Y.: Parker Publishing Co., Inc., 1966. This person became a successful business executive. His focus is to help you develop your ESP.

MASTERS, ROBERT and HOUSTON, JEAN. *Mind Games: The Guide to Inner Space.* New York: Dell Books, Inc., 1972. A how-to book of mental exercises for achieving altered states of consciousness. Often called the yoga of the West.

MAY, ROLLO. *The Courage to Create.* New York: Bantam Books, Inc., 1975. If you know how to be creative, you need to get in touch with your intuition. You need to be courageous to do either.

RAUDSEPP, EUGENE with HOUGH, GEORGE P. JR. *Creative Growth Games.* New York: Perigee Books, 1977. Games to practice and develop your creativity. You need to get in touch with both sides of your brain to do it.

RAUDSEPP, EUGENE. *How Creative Are You?* New York: Perigee Books: 1981. The third in the series. Best to read this book and then use the other two for exercises since it gives you an overview and test of your creativity.

RAUDSEPP, EUGENE. *More Creative Growth Games.* New York: Perigee Books, 1980. Second in the three-part series of game books all for the same purpose.

ROBERTS, JANE. *How to Develop Your ESP Power.* New York: Frederick Fell Publishers, Inc., 1980 printing. Another primer on psychic phenomena.

ROZMAN, DEBORAH. *Meditation for Children.* Milbrae, Calif.: Celestial Arts, 1976. Tells you how to meditate with your family, your children, and yourself. Great for us all.

SCHEMEL, GEORGE J. and BORBELY, JAMES A. *Facing Your Type.* Wernersville, Pa.: Typofile Press, 1982. This is designed to complement the MBTI in understanding and interpreting your personality type and abilities, including intuition. A step for developing your intuition is understanding yourself.

SCOTT, IAN, ed. *The Luscher Color Test: The Remarkable Test That Reveals Your Personality Through Color.* New York: Pocket Books, 1969. Translated from the original German, this test is an excellent deep psychological test that can be used both for diagnosis and also for developing one's intuitive ability. Based on your preference for basic colors and the order therein.

STEADMAN, ALICE. *Who's the Matter With Me?* Marina del Ray, Calif.: DeVorss & Co., 1969. Gives you a good understanding of the relationship between your health and your mind. Think about it.

THURSTON, MARK A. *Understand and Develop Your ESP.* Virginia Beach, Va.: ARE Press, 1977. Development of your psychic abilities following methods Edgar Cayce outlined for you.

WEINSTEIN, MATT and GOODMAN, JOEL. *Playfair: Everybody's Guide to Noncompetitive Play.* San Luis Obispo, Calif.: Impact Publishers, 1980. A guide to the new age of noncompetitive games that can be used in workshops in various organizational settings.

WILLIAMS, PAUL. *Das Energi.* New York: Electra Books, 1973. A book to read and reread periodically. It will help you understand you, everyone, and everything else. It will help you develop your intuition.

Articles

AGOR, WESTON H. "Training Public Managers to Develop and Use Their Intuition for Decision Making." In *Professional Development Handbook, 1983,* edited by Kent T. Higgins. Washington, D.C.: American Society for Public Administration, 1983. Reports results of nationally testing a random sample of public administrators and outlines how to develop their intuitive ability through a training program using many of the materials outlined above and in this book.

EVERETT, ED. "Improving Creativity—One Organization's Approach." *Public Management* (February, 1983), pp. 7–8. This government organization worked on developing their mental capital through the use of the Raudsepp book series noted above.

VAUGHAN, ALAN. "Intuition, Precognition, and the Art of Prediction." *The Futurist* (June, 1982), pp. 5–10. Describes many of the practical applications of intuition and recent research on Psi phenomenon. Also gives you exercises on how to practice your ability to see the future.

VON OECH, ROGER. "The Mind As a Management Tool." *Public Management* (January, 1982), pp. 7–12. Keys to opening the intuition are outlined.

Tests and Exercises

As outlined in Chapters 3 and 4, these tests and exercises can be used along with the other materials described to implement an overall program for developing and using your intuition to manage organizations.

BODUCH, ROBERT, and others. *Manual for The Project Planning Situation: An Experience in Team Planning, 3d ed.* Plymouth, Mich.: Human Synergistics, 1975. Can be used to show how you as an individual and in a group think and solve problems.

LAFFERTY, J. CLAYTON. *Level 1: Life Styles: Interpretation Manual.* Plymouth, Mich.: Human Synergistics, 1980. Tells you how to think and act and how likely you are to be effective in an organizational setting based on test results. Manual relates tests to other organizational research. Knowing yourself in this way is the key to developing your potential.

SCHUTZ, WILL. *FIRO Awareness Scales Manual.* Palo Alto, Calif.: Consulting Psychologists Press, 1978. Describes how to use his test on needs for inclusion, control, and affection. Intuitive types tend to score high on affection and inclusion, while control types score higher in left brain skills. The manual is particularly useful for occupational score data.

SCHUTZ, WILL. *Trainers Manual for The Schutz Measures: An Integrated System for Assessing Elements of Awareness.* San Diego, Calif.: University Associates, Inc., 1982. His newest series of tests that measure elements of behavior, feelings, self-concept, relationships, and job. Together with his newest book *Profound Simplicity,* which is available from the same outlet, you have a powerful package that can be used to tap into and develop your intuitive skills.

Audio-Visual Materials/Video Tapes

AGOR, WESTON H. and Center for Professional Development, College of Business, University of Texas at El Paso. "How to Develop Your Intuition for Management." El Paso, Tex.: University Television Productions, 1983. This is a 1-hour tape of a presentation to 130 Chamber of Commerce executives. Available from author, ENFP Enterprises, Inc., 6022 Caprock, #103, El Paso, TX 79912.

AGOR, WESTON H. and VAUGHAN, ALAN. "Intuitive Management." Hollywood, Calif.: UMS Television Productions, 1982. Personal interview on the television program "Quest Four" by Damien Simpson. The 1-hour tape explains how intuition can be developed and used to make decisions. Available from author (same address).

AGOR, WESTON H. and Walt Disney Enterprises. "Using Intuition to be More Effective at Work and in Your Personal Life." Glendale, Calif.: WED Enterprises, 1982. Two-hour videotape production based on presentation to managers and staff in WED Forum, August 12, 1982. Available from author, ENFP Enterprises, Inc., 6022 Caprock, Apt. 103, El Paso, TX 79912.

Numerous tapes on developing various aspects of your intuitive ability available from such organizations as ARE (Virginia Beach, Va.), University of the Trees (Boulder Creek, Calif.), and Potentials Unlimited (Grand Rapids, Mich.).

5. INNOVATIVE USE OF INTUITION IN MODERN ORGANIZATIONS

There are a number of organizations and programs now working on the frontier of applying the use of intuition and other psychic skills to management. Educational institutions are now also experimenting in this area. Below are some selected programs for your own review and assessment.

Books, Catalogues, and Programs

AGOR, WESTON H. *ENFP Enterprises.* El Paso, Tex.: ENFP Enterprises, 1983. Explains the services the organization provides including testing for intuition, organizational consulting, training, and publications available. This brochure outlines the basic thrust of the organization and what it can do for you. Available from author (same address).

"American Leadership Forum: Executive Summary." Houston, Tex.: American Leadership Forum, 1983. Devoted to the encouragement and development of more responsible and effective public leadership for the good of all people. They select fellows for leadership training to meet future challenges. Their 1983 program, which was presented by Innovation Associates (see below), included training in the use of intuition.

"Brain Technology Corporation." Richardson, Tex., 1983. Headed by Dudley Lynch, this organization uses different brain styles and research to train management to be more effective. They also publish a newsletter entitled *Brain & Strategy.*

"Center for Creative Leadership." Greensboro, NC, 1983. Teaches innovative and creative approaches to problem solving. Among approaches used is emphasis on inductive thinking.

GOODSPEED, BENNETT W., Partner of Inferential Focus. New York, 1983. Besides his own firm's activities, which specialize in the use of intuitive techniques of analysis, he formed before his recent death a "Right Hemisphere Club" of executives to network and support intuitive approaches to problem solving. He also taught an innovative course at Manhattansville College entitled "Intuition and Business."

"Innovation Associates." Framingham, Mass., 1983. Specialize in the use of intuition in management and training for the integration of intuitive and analytical skills. They see metanoic organizations as the wave of the future where people transcend their personal identity and become linked to a higher purpose. The intuitive-integrative leader is the engine to this movement.

KAPCHAN, JACK A. "Parapsychology." Coral Gables, Fla.: University of Miami, 1983. A psychologist at The University, he offers a very innovative course on parapsychology including introduction to altered states of consciousness and major sources for further work in the field of the psychic.

"Ned Herrmann: Applied Creative Services." Lake Lure, N.C., 1983. Herrmann originally ran the "Applied Creative Thinking Workshop" at The Management Development Institute in Crotonville, New York. He specializes in workshops that focus on creative thinking using the research on brain hemispheres. This won Roger Sperry the Nobel Prize. An artist, he also emphasizes the use of multimedia in his work.

"Psychic Enterprises, Inc." Los Angeles, Calif., 1983. Relying on the psychic ability of a team of associates, Psychic Enterprises, Inc. provide advisory management services to clients.

RAY, MICHEL and MYERS, ROCHELLE. "Creativity in Business." Stanford, Calif.: Graduate School of Business, Stanford University, 1983. One of the more innovative experimental courses currently available in main line management education programs across the country. Includes introduction to numerous inductive techniques. See also articles cited below.

"The Institute for Futures Forecasting." Carmel, Calif., 1983. Headed by David Loye, it conducts research on brain styles and their relationship to one's ability to project the future.

"The University for Humanistic Studies." San Diego, Calif., 1983. Provides a total formal course program in humanistic psychology, holistic health, consciousness, and acupuncture.

VAUGHAN, ALAN. *The Edge of Tomorrow: How to Foresee and Fulfill Your Future.* New York: Coward, McCaun & Geoghegan, 1982. Works on using intuition to foresee the future. Here, he tells you how to develop your talents, too. Vaughan is considered nationally as one of the most accurate predictors—by such organizations as Central Premonitions Registry.

"World University in Ojai." Ojai, Calif., 1983. They offer a formal program of study including ethics, arts and crafts, and the arts of psychology, including intuitive awareness programs.

Articles

AGOR, WESTON H. "Management in the Future: Using Intuitive Thinking." *Real Estate Business* (Summer, 1983), pp. 14–17 and 27. Describes how using intuition to make management decisions will have particular relevance as a survival skill in the real estate industry.

AGOR, WESTON H. "Tomorrow's Intuitive Leader," *The Futurist* (August, 1983, pp. 4{–53). Outlines why intuition will be a premium management skill in the future, how to test for it, develop it, and use it to make decisions.

AGOR, WESTON H. "Using Intuition to Manage Organizations." *The Bureaucrat: The Journal for Public Managers* (Winter, 1983–4), Vol. 12, No. 4, pp. 49–52. In this special issue on trends in public administration, this article explains how using intuition will be a particularly useful skill for coping with the future changes emerging.

AGOR, WESTON H. "Using Intuition to Manage Organizations in the Future." *Business Horizons* (July, 1984) forthcoming. This article points out that a successful top manager in the future will need to possess intuitive skills as well as analytical skills in order to survive successfully. It also argues for the implementation of training programs in "right brain" skills in order to prepare managers for the future.

BARADAT DE VALLE, MARIA ELENA. "La Intuicion: Explorando El Sexto Sentido." *Harpers Bazaar En Espanol* (June, 1983), pp. 70–71 and 103. Magazine interview with me concerning my work and workshops on intuition conducted in Miami, Fla.

BERG, ERIC N. "Zen and the Stanford Business Student: Creativity Skills Are Taught by Way of I Ching and Chanting. But the Aim is Serious." *The New York Times* (January 30, 1983), p. 9. Describes the Ray and Myers creativity class previously noted.

CARROLL, JERRY. "Over-Achievers Swarm to This Exotic Class: MBA's Who Meditate, Chant and Read Tarot Cards." *San Francisco Chronicle* (February 17, 1983), p. 46. Tells more about Ray and Myers class noted above.

COLLIGAN, DOUGLAS. "Your Gift of Prophecy." *Reader's Digest* (September, 1982), pp. 145–150. Discusses the use of group intuition to predict the future.

"Going for It: Who Are Today's New Magnates, New Moguls, New Wheeler-Dealers, New Builders of Business Empires: Well, They're Women." *Southwest Airline Magazine* (June, 1983), pp. 75 on. Discusses the success of a number of up and coming women executives from the Southwest. They have "new age" characteristics in common—a vision, a philosophy of life and work that governs their every move. They are all creative, and have found new solutions to old problems.

"Harvard's Bok Urges Changing 'Expensive, Inefficient' Legal System, Seeks Law-School Curriculum Reform." *The Chronicle of Higher Education* (May 4, 1983), pp. 8–9. Asks legal educators to get off the left side and start taking into account the other half of their brain too. Also predicts the future—he seems on target.

HAYES, THOMAS C. "Celestial Seasonings Pins Its Hopes on More than Herbal Tea." *The New York Times* (April 3, 1983), pp. 6–7. Tells how the cofounder of this firm feels he can succeed employing a higher level of consciousness than has often been characterized by business.

Leading Edge Bulletin. Los Angeles, Calif.: Interface Press, Inc. A newsletter issued every three weeks on innovative applications in organizations that are transforming the world around us.

LOYE, DAVID. "Let George Do It: A New Look at Business Forecasting." *Management Review* (May, 1978), pp. 48–52. Condensed summary of his book, *The Knowable Future,* cited above.

MAGNUSON, ROBERT. "Battered in 1981, Economic Forecasters Resolve to Do Better in 1982." *Los Angeles Times* (January 3, 1982), pp. 1 and 4. Left-brain economic projections appear to be off the wall despite all the facts and all the computers.

MALABRE JR., ALFRED L. "If One Economist Goofs, Will 46 Do Any Better? Robert Eggert Thinks So, and He May Be Right." *The Wall Street Journal* (April 6, 1983), p. 50. Consensus forecasting appears to work better than going it alone. Intuition and synergy at work.

MCGINLEY, LAURIE. "Forecasters Overhaul 'Models' of Economy in Wake of 1982 Errors." *The Wall Street Journal* (February 17, 1983), p. 1. Despite their promise to do better in 1982, they didn't. Maybe that should tell us something.

NAUTON, ENA. "Brain Wars: Which Side Are You On? The Right Side Just Might Be a Life Saver." *The Miami Herald* (February 20, 1983), Living Today Section, pp. 1 and 8. Summarizes the work on brain theory and my own workshop on intuitive management at The University of Miami and elsewhere across the country.

Reincarnation Report. Malibus, Calif., 1983. Monthly journal edited until June, 1983 by Alan Vaughan. Under his editorship it was a good place to go for cutting edge applications in the Psi field. If Patton thought he was, maybe he was.

ROSE, FRANK. "The Mass Production of Engineers: The Future is Being Designed by Engineers. The One Thing We Know About the Future Is That It's More Complicated Than That." *Esquire Magazine* (May, 1983), pp. 74–84. Discusses the need to change the way we are training our engineers to have both judgment as well as technical expertise.

TANNER, MARCIA. "Michael Ray Unlocks Creativity in Business School Class." *Campus Report* (December 8, 1982), pp. 13 and 17. More on Ray and Myers' class involving executive quotes on the use of intuition in their management.

TYRRELL, JR., R. EMMETT. "Recovery Unutterable for Economic 'Gurus'."

Sun-Sentinel (March 11, 1983), p. 19. Why do we pay so much for these economic projections if they are so bad?

"Visions: Report on Cal State's Future Raises Doubts." *Los Angeles Times* (February 6, 1983), pp. 1 and 22. Among other things, this report acknowledges that intuition and ESP may be ways of training effectively—maybe more so than what we are doing now.

WILLS, KENDALL J. "An Explorer Charts the Passages of the Executive Mind." *The New York Times* (March 6, 1983), Business Section. Efforts to chart how top executives think by Abraham Zaleznik at Harvard Business School.

Tests and Exercises

"The 1983 Knowable Future Study." Carmel, Calif.: The Institute for Futures Forecasting, 1983. National survey and test instrument that David Loye is using to try and correlate brain styles with ability to predict the future. Available from the author at 25700 Shaffer Way, Carmel, Ca. 93923.

VAUGHAN, ALAN. "The Psychic Defender." Software computer game developed for use on the Apple microcomputer. Enables you to practice and develop your intuitive skills. Available along with his book, *The Edge of Tomorrow,* from the author at Enterprising Ideas, 111 E. Broadway, Suite 18, Glendale, California 91205.

Index